Where's Your Bucket?

Where's Your
Bucket?

Dana Neubert

BOB PROCTOR
LIFE
SUCCESS
PUBLISHING

LIFESUCCESS PUBLISHING, LLC
8900 E Pinnacle Peak Road, Suite D240
Scottsdale, AZ 85255

Telephone:	800.473.7134
Fax:	480.661.1014
E-mail:	admin@lifesuccesspublishing.com
ISBN:	978-1-59930-132-7
Cover:	Erick Sellers & LifeSuccess Publishing
Layout:	Erick Sellers & LifeSuccess Publishing

COMPANIES, ORGANIZATIONS, INSTITUTIONS, AND INDUSTRY PUBLICATIONS: Quantity discounts are available on bulk purchases of this book for reselling, educational purposes, subscription incentives, gifts, sponsorship, or fundraising. Special books or book excerpts can also be created to fit specific needs such as private labeling with your logo on the cover and a message from a VIP printed inside. For more information please contact our Special Sales Department at LifeSuccess Publishing.

Testimonials

"Where's Your Bucket? teaches us to take charge of our lives and succeed."
— **Cindy Nelson, author of *If Not Now, When?***

"This book will set a new standard for what is possible in your life."
— **Muriel Stickney, author of *Life's Journey***

"A must read for anyone who is struggling to find their own path to financial freedom."
— **David Ogunnaike, author of *The Millionaire Genius***

"Dana jump starts your success vehicle with this book."
— **James Geiger MD., author of *The Sweet Smell of Success***

"This book is necessary in anyone's bookcase who wants to live the life of their dreams."
— **Gerry Robert, author of *The Millionaire Mindset***

"In Where's Your Bucket?, Dana shows readers how to start living by taking control of your life."
— **Sally Walker, author of** *The Good Life Triangle*

"Dana encourages readers to step out of the norm and achieve their highest potential."
— **Bob Proctor, author of** *You Were Born Rich*
and featured in *"The Secret"*

"Where's Your Bucket? is the key to personal growth and financial success."
— **Oddmund Berger, author of** *Your Life's Echo*

"With each turn of a page, you are empowered more and more."
— **Dean Storer, author of** *The Make it Happen Man*

"Dana's tremendous success within her own life serves as an example for the rest of us."
— **Mary Ellen Lapp, author of** *The Color of Success*

Acknowledgments and Dedications

This book is dedicated to my family and friends for all of their encouragement and support. Thank you for all of your kind words and positive thoughts. You helped to make my dream a reality.

I was blessed to have the support of many special people and would like to take this opportunity to say thank you. To Mary, who shared my vision for this book and gave me guidance and insight throughout this project, I thank you. I want to thank both my children Nicole and Gabe, who are both unique in their own way. You have taught me just as much about life as I have taught you.

Foreword

Dana Neubert's *Where's Your Bucket?* is the most promising strategy I've seen for sustained, substantive personal and financial improvement by developing the ability to function at your highest potential. Each chapter in this book has been chosen purposefully. Dana is someone with expertise in her field, an individual who has not only pursued her dreams relentlessly, but who is also expected to remain current in the ever-evolving world of business and finance.

Much has been written about improving your life and gaining financial independence, but nothing compares to *Where's Your Bucket?* Dana's insights create an environment for the reader that fosters emotional support and personal growth. Her words will encourage and inspire you to achieve what you never thought possible. This book offers specific and practical recommendations for anyone who seeks to transform his or her life and is an absolute must-read.

– **Gerry Robert, author of *The Millionaire Mindset***

Table of Contents

Introduction

What keeps us from having what we truly desire? Why are so many of us stuck in a career with no hope of advancement? Why do we go through life thinking that we can't possibly live up to our potential? So many of us search for answers and struggle with these issues. Life is full of opportunities; all you need is a bucket to carry them in. Why spend your time gazing down into the darkness of an empty bucket, when you have the ability to reap the benefits of all that life has to offer and fill your bucket until it overflows. Now is the time to step back, take a look at yourself and realize the unlimited possibilities for success available to fill your bucket in life. We all are born with the same bucket; it is just a matter of what you choose to put in yours.

In *Where's Your Bucket?* I reveal the lessons I have learned on the journey of finding my passion and getting the most out of life. I describe the limiting behaviors that we fall into and show you how to recognize them. You will understand how all of your negative beliefs from the past have prevented you from living the life you deserve. Once you overcome the fear of changing yourself, you will, for the first time, be able to understand how those similar fears prevent you from financial success.

Success can be a frightening prospect when you consider that you may have to take risks in life. But the willingness to take risks and think differently is the key ingredient in every success, whether it is personal or financial. Learning to take a challenge head-on gives you a feeling of self-confidence that trickles into every aspect of your life. Accomplishment follows accomplishment, building a new sense of self along the way. We begin to dream again and to imagine for the first time a life of fulfillment.

The message of *Where's Your Bucket?* is that there is unlimited abundance for each of us, and we are capable of living the life we desire.

"Nobody is lazy; they just haven't found their passion."

Unknown

Chapter One

Finding Your Passion in Life

Chapter One

Finding Your Passion in Life

What is your passion in life? This is a very thought-provoking question for most of us. For some, it can also be an uncomfortable one as well. You can search for these answers in many different places, from the latest self–help books, to seeking a friend's advice. But in all reality, you are the only one who can answer this question. Delving inside ourselves to search for our passion takes us on a path to self-discovery. The answer to this question can give you peace, purpose and power to change.

"First say to yourself what would you be . . . then do what you have to do."

Epictetus

Imagine for a moment that you're building a house. You hire a contractor, but he never consults the architects' blueprints. He works without a plan. Would this make you nervous? How can he build your house without knowing where to lay the foundation, erect the walls and place the windows? After all is said and done, your new home won't look anything like your original idea. Will you be satisfied? Of course not!

The same can be said of life. How can we try to build our life without first finding our true passion? Without this important "blueprint," we are living our life on a whim. Once we find our passion, everything works together for the good of the universe. True fulfillment and meaning in life is gained by living according to your passion.

By answering this question and making the answer the center of your life, you will discover the very purpose for which you were created. There is nothing and no one else who can do this--no religion, no philosophy, no person. Just you.

For years, I lived on autopilot. I ate, breathed, shopped, studied and generally went through life without knowing why I did what I did, why I even existed. I made decisions based on how I felt at the time.

Still, the deeper questions of life haunted me. "Why am I here?" I wondered. "Who am I? Where do I want to go? And how can I get there?" No matter where I turned, the answers eluded me.

A Statement for Passion

In pursuit of my passion, I reached a turning point when I realized that at the end of my life, I would not be asked, "Why were you not Nelson Mandela or Mother Teresa?" But instead, I would be asked, "Why were you not Dana Neubert?" Since each of us is unique, it's safe to assume that each of us also has our own passion, a reason for being that is uniquely personal.

"The thing is to understand myself, to see what God really wants me to do; the thing is to find a truth which is true for me, to find the idea for which I can live or die."

Søren Kierkegaard

I have always thought that my life should have meaning, though I never thought meaning could be found every minute of every day. I mean, really, how meaningful is cooking dinner and cleaning house? Life shouldn't just be about work; we need a little fun every now and then. But life has to be more than just pleasure-seeking, partly because the enjoyment doesn't last. It's here for a moment, then gone. Your life should be a balance between the two.

Passion is different from pleasure. For one, it doesn't necessarily involve extraordinary accomplishments. Instead, it often comes forth as a commitment to be faithful in even the most undervalued tasks. Knowing and fulfilling your life's passion brings you to a place of enthusiasm and excitement. It is the best place for you to be.

Your passion is the essence of who you are. It is the reason you are alive. To know your passion, you first have to know who you are. Don't let culture, skills or intelligence limit you in your search for passion. Instead, look at these as clues as to why you were born in such a place and at such a time.

Take me, for example. I was ten years old when I first said I wanted to go to the Olympics. I loved sports, especially volleyball. I would spend hours in the gym practicing volleys and spikes. With each ball I served, I marveled at what it would be like to stand in front of a crowd of tens of thousands of spectators who were watching me lead my team to victory. In my senior year of high school, my coach gave me nothing but discouraging comments and negative feedback. One night after we lost one of our games, he told me that I was a terrible player and responsible for the team's loss. Although his words had little practical value to me at the time, I look back now and realize that he actually taught me a lesson. Don't listen to anyone's comments. I could have gone to the Olympics, but instead I let his words keep me from my dream. Today I know that forgoing my dream was my fault, not his, and I will never let anyone tell me that I can't do something. I now have confidence in my abilities to fulfill my dreams.

As soon as I found myself investing in my first piece of real estate, something inside me clicked. I knew for the first time in my life that I was doing what I was meant to do. Best of all, I couldn't believe I was getting paid for it! The fulfillment I experienced helped take me one step further, developing a personal mission statement. Large corporations and small businesses have a mission statement to help them stay on track, so why shouldn't I?

"The things which matter most must never be at the mercy of things which matter least."

Goethe

In one short, succinct, powerful and inspiring sentence, I could tell the world what I was really about. This statement covered my personal life, my work life, my social life and my spiritual life. Your personal mission statement is a very important part in fulfilling your passion. It gives you the readiness to follow your heart and your dreams. In the gray box on the next page, write, in one statement, what your purpose is- or what you want it to be!

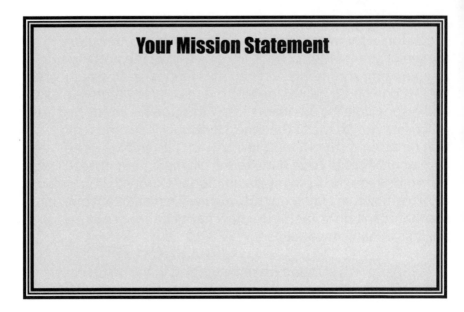

Mapping Your Mission Statement

Having a mission statement alone isn't enough. You also have to have a strategic plan set in place. Living without a mission is no different than taking off on a vacation without a map. You know your destination, and you may even know a general direction to go. Eventually you will get there, but how many U-turns do you have to make along the journey? How much time would you have saved if you followed the directions from a map?

Your mission statement map should include a set of goals and the best means to accomplish them. These goals need to be specific and cover all aspects of your life as well as any potential challenges. With these goals on paper, you will have a much clearer picture of where your life is heading. Pick and choose what you like to learn more about, what you enjoy and what you're gifted in.

Take a moment and think briefly about your current goals. Can you clearly articulate them? Will achieving your goals bring a true sense of satisfaction and fulfillment? It's possible to successfully achieve all of your goals and still not find your passion in life. There's a major difference between accomplishing your goals and fulfilling your passion.

Therefore, it's crucial to look beyond your short-term goals and examine your passion, which you'll have for a lifetime. When you look, what do you see? You may find that you are going through life, wondering what it's all about or wondering what will provide you with lasting fulfillment.

"I've never transcended what I haven't embraced."
Jon Marc Hammer

If this sounds familiar, you are more than likely pursuing goals for success rather than pursuing your passion. For one reason, it's much easier. Most of us have been urged to fulfill goals since we were children. We learn to ride our bikes without training wheels, get an "A" in history, we may even make the varsity team. Many of us have achieved quite a lot throughout our lives.

While most of us have goals that we work to achieve, only a few of us have found our passion in life. Only in the realization of our goals does passion ring true. Our goals are objectives we achieve, but our passion answers the questions, "Why am I here?" and "Where am I going?" Without passion, how can we know if we have meaningful goals? Jobs and values do not produce passion; instead, passion helps form our careers and values.

Fulfilling Our Passions in Life

Of course, fulfilling your passion in life takes time. It requires an open mind and a willingness to listen and learn. The universe presents us with many opportunities to follow our passion. We just have to open ourselves up to the idea. In fact, once you align yourself with the universe and forge a deep understanding with what it has in store for you, you will soon experience real passion in your life. You will soon come to live in harmony. You will no longer measure success by what you do; your success will be measured by who you are.

Our passion comes into our lives if we ask. It is created uniquely for each of us for the purpose of fulfilling us. Not only does our passion impart true and lasting meaning, but it gives us power for living life and fulfilling that passion, and it connects us to true satisfaction.

The most important and the most difficult part of fulfilling your passion is actually doing it. Action is required to manifest your dreams. You have to take a leap of faith. Don't worry that something may not work out as planned. In all reality, it probably won't, but that's okay. Use the experience as a learning tool and move yourself forward with your newfound knowledge. Remember that everything in the universe happens for a reason. You can't wait for the assurance that nothing will go wrong. You have to take risks in order to live a life of passion and fulfillment.

Following your passion takes commitment and perseverance. It won't be easy, yet there is no better hope than reaching the end of your life and being able to say, "I have lived fully. I have lived my passion."

"Whether you think you can or you think you can't your right"

Henry Ford

Chapter Two

Affirm Your Future

Chapter Two

Affirm Your Future

Do you realize that every thought you think and every word you say is an affirmation? What's the difference in the psychology of a loser and a winner, someone one who is full of stress and someone who is relaxed, someone who is angry and someone who is calm, someone who is worried and someone who is confident? The difference is attributed to how you view situations and what you say to yourself. Your outcomes are predetermined by your beliefs, and your beliefs are influenced by your visions and your self-talk.

Affirmations are all of your self-talk or inner dialogue. You are constantly affirming yourself subconsciously with your words and thoughts, and this flow of affirmations is creating your life experiences. Every affirmation you think or say is a reflection of your current inner facts or beliefs. Many of these "inner facts" may not actually be the truth of who you really are or may be based on invalid impressions you developed as a child. If examined as an adult, these can be exposed as incorrect. Well, forget about the past! Focus on the future and move mountains with me.

Positive affirmations are designed to challenge all of your negative beliefs. Affirmations aren't just statements repeated over and over. The proper use of affirmations involves a process of becoming aware of your thoughts and words in everyday life and changing negative thoughts into happy and productive thoughts.

Your subconscious mind assumes what it has been fed to be the truth. It also uses the behavioral patterns you have learned to instantly react to everyday events in your life. This is essential for survival. Your learned reactions and thought patterns allow you to automatically react to circumstances, particularly in times of danger or when there is no time for consideration. This automatic response can be inappropriate if your belief system has formed a skewed perspective of who you really are. More often than not, your beliefs aren't aligned so that you can live a passion-filled life. Wallace D. Wattles once said, "To think according to appearances is easy. To think truth regardless of appearances is laborious and requires the expenditure of more power than any other work a person has to perform. . . . To think what you want to think is to think truth regardless of appearances."

Using positive affirmations will help you to undermine and replace false beliefs with positive and self-nurturing beliefs. Positive affirmations are usually short positive statements which you repeat to yourself. Please note that the words you use in conversation must match these affirmations, or you will create internal conflict. To yourself you say you are a financial giant, but to others you say that you are doing well. Affirmations are much stronger and useful when they match all of your dialogue, internal and external.

The concept is quite simple. By filling your bucket with negative talk, you are painting the canvas of your mind with self-deprecating doubt. On the other hand, by filling your bucket with positive dialogue, you have a beautiful canvas bursting with positive and creative energy.

These statements must be worded very carefully. Remember that everything you say and think is an affirmation. The more determined you are to make and accept change, the better positive affirmations will work for you. Positive affirmation statements help you to define and live your passion. Read this true story to see what I mean.

I lent a man $100,000 to remodel his home. He could not pay me back, so I had to buy the house he was remodeling. His home is 10,000 sq. ft. and is valued at 2.6 million dollars. I was going to buy this home and then immediately sell it to a very famous Denver Bronco football player the next day. A week before the closing, my partner and I were going through the house. I turned to her and asked if she would like to move in. She looked at me like I was crazy and mumbled something about how we couldn't ever afford the $11,000 a month mortgage.

I said, "That's not what I asked you. I asked if you would like to live here." She thought for a moment and told me how she would love to live here and have family get togethers in this home as she comes from a very large family. I told myself that we will live in this house. One week later we moved in. I had no idea how we would pay for the mortgage, but I repeated my positive affirmation and was confident that a way would be shown. That decision changed my life. I now know that you can have and do anything in this world if you truly believe.

Our bills now are over $30,000 a month and they are easier to make than when they were $300 a month.

Repeating, and more importantly, feeling affirmations works by creating a deep, lasting impression in your subconscious mind. The more repetition and feeling you can give to these, the deeper the impression. The following are a few guidelines for creating positive affirmations:

- Keep your affirmations to concise, specific and simple language.
- Only use positive statements. Never use words such as can't, won't, not, maybe, one day, and so forth.
- Keep your affirmations in the present tense, stated as if you have already received what you want.
  Use the gray box on the following page to create your own affirmations.

Start by taking some time to think about areas in your life you would like to change and how you want your life to be. Write down the most important ones in a list. After you've written them down, write out a couple of positive statements for each one. Remember to concentrate on what you want out of life, not want you don't want out of life. And dream big! Don't worry about how the dream will be achieved; simply write down the dream. Here is one of my affirmations as an example:

Add "I am so happy and grateful now that I have increased my income to $50,000 a month."

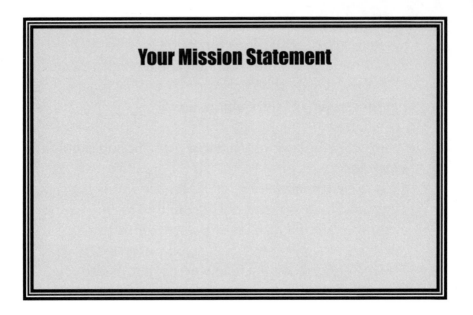

Now that you've planted your affirmations in your mind, visualize them in image form. Then, attach belief to that image. Believe completely with your heart and mind that what you want is possible for you.

"What the mind of man can conceive and believe, it can achieve."
Napoleon Hill

Visualization is the process of creating pictures in your mind. Visualization is an idea, a thought form, in picture. Your subconscious mind thinks in terms of pictures. Creating a picture allows you to take a shortcut directly into your subconscious. Visualization creates a belief that can alter the circumstances of your life.

Through visualization, you can deliver direct messages into your subconscious mind, and the most helpful truth about the subconscious mind is that it does not know the difference between "reality" and images. Scientists have tested Olympic athletes by hooking them up to a series of electronic devices and having the athletes "run the race in their mind" using visualization. These scientists have found that the muscles and nerves in the athletes fired as if they were actually running, even though they were sitting in a chair.

Your subconscious mind, therefore, does not have the ability to rationalize. Whatever you consistently tell your subconscious mind is taken as the truth. So, in essence, if you consistently picture yourself as having already achieved your purpose, your subconscious mind will soon believe that it to be true. The work of your subconscious mind is to balance your inner and outer reality. In order to do so, it sets into motion any necessary actions you need to take to create in the physical realm that which you believe in your mind to be true. Training your subconscious mind to accept your purpose and believing it to be true will turn your purpose into a reality.

You can do the visualization activity virtually anywhere, but a quiet, safe place where you will not be disturbed is best. Ensure that you are totally relaxed and calm, ready to live your dream. If you find it hard to relax, take ten slow, deep breaths, concentrating on the air flowing into your lungs and flowing out of your lungs. Now, focus your mind on what you want to do, have or be. Keep replaying the internal film of yourself actually doing, having or being it. The more you do this exercise, the stronger it will become and the quicker your subconscious mind will move you into the right actions to achieve it.

Think of something you want to try this technique on. Concentrate and imagine yourself in the situation; be realistic about the experience, and keep it true to how you expect it to be. See yourself doing everything right. Imagine yourself as though watching a movie through others' eyes, seeing yourself succeed.

If you have problems visualizing a successful outcome, run through your internal picture again, and step into the bodies of others observing you. What do they see? What do they think?

Visualization can give you insight into potential challenges. Many of these can simply be overcome by repainting your inner picture; others may highlight a basic reality that may help you realign your immediate goals or expectations.

An effective visualization happens when you make the pictures in your mind real. Think of visualizations as movies constantly playing in your mind. Fill your visualizations with emotion and energy. The more realistic they appear to you, the more they are becoming a reality. You have to feel the joy of achieving your goal, smell the smells and hear the sounds. When possible, say your affirmations out loud. Adding a lot of emotion to your voice is powerful, so say it like you mean it!

Affirmations and visualizations combined are powerful tools that will help you create a belief and hold a vision that will lead you to your goals and subsequently your life's purpose. Visualize your affirmations as living pictures of truth.

In this way, you can begin to create the reality you desire. Use the suggestions on the following page to help you harness the power for both affirmations and visualizations:

- Use as many senses as possible in affirmations and visualizations. Verbalize statements out loud after writing them down. Listen to yourself say these statements while standing in front of a mirror. When you visualize your performance, recreate as much of the scene as possible to create an accurate simulation. Imagine what it sounds like, what it feels like, what it smells like, and so forth.

- Make affirmations and visualizations emotional. Imagine what it will feel like to be happy, successful, powerful and self-assured. Visualize yourself experiencing these emotions. At the same time, work to eliminate statements of negative emotions from your life, such as, "I'm tired, I'm sad/depressed, I'm lonely, I'm bored, I'm overwhelmed." There are times when I feel that I am too tired to do my "reprogramming," but once I get started, I get into the feeling place of this powerful tool, and at the end I feel amazing. I stand taller and straighter and have an immovable grin on my face.

No matter who you are or what your career is, affirmations and visualizations will improve your life. If used correctly, they will change the way you think, reprogram your mind, and remove old negative beliefs that have sabotaged you throughout your life. You will achieve the life you've always wanted.

"It's your thoughts behind the words you speak that create your attitude."

Jeffery Gitomer

Chapter Three

Attitude is Everything

Chapter Three

Attitude is Everything

I was married for eighteen years and have two children. I got divorced three years ago and was left with nothing. I knew I didn't want a nine- to- five job. So I moved in with my friend who had a job. She had worked for the same company for seventeen years, and one day she came home crying. When I asked her why, she told me they gave her a bad evaluation. I told her to quit, and she said, "I can't. Who will pay the mortgage?" I told her that I had no idea, but unless we are desperate, we will do nothing. So she quit the next day. Very soon after that, I learned what it was like to be desperate. We borrowed from credit cards to pay bills. I finally got a brilliant idea to borrow $10,000 on my credit card to buy fifty of those quarter vending machines. I thought we were going to be rich doing this. My partner always said, "Yep, one quarter at a time!" Unfortunately, we didn't do so well and ended up selling them.

Then came yet another one of my brilliant ideas. I love animals, so I thought we could become pet-sitters. It was a great business, but I realized we were trading our time for money. However, while watching late night TV realized we could become rich in real estate while I was taking care of the animals and watching late night TV. How crazy is that?

In two and a half years, my partner and I owned over eleven million dollars in real estate. Because we are willing to take risks and make mistakes, we are successful. Failure has never been an option. When something doesn't work and that door closes, it just means another door has opened. How you live each day is not dictated by the circumstances of that day. It is dictated by how you handle those circumstances. You choose each morning to face the day with a positive outlook or a negative one. You only have a bad day if you allow yourself to view it as such. I know that may sound over-simplistic, but the truth is that having a good attitude is very simplistic. We all go wrong when we let our inner voice convince us that we must have a certain set of circumstances to have a positive outlook.

We could think that we'll have a great attitude and positive outlook when we achieve some of the following:

- Get a promotion.
- Make a million dollars.
- Find the right soul mate.
- Buy a bigger house or car.
- Get out of debt.
- Lose weight.
- Get a college degree.

The sad thing is that none of these things will make us happy or give us a positive attitude about your life. Why? Because things don't bring happiness. They don't bring happiness to me, and they won't bring happiness to you, either. These may all be goals for your life, but you can choose to be happy and positive now as you are reaching for those goals, rather than bitter and despondent because they seem so far away.

"Human beings, by changing the inner attitudes of their minds, can change the outer aspects of their lives."
William James

So the key is to squelch the inner voice and convince yourself that you are worthy of the same respect as someone who has reached every goal on the list above. The fact that you're not quite there yet doesn't diminish you as a person in any way, and therefore, shouldn't affect your view of the world.

"The greatest discovery of my generation is that a human being can alter his life by altering his attitude and mind."
William James

Many people take every setback or obstacle personally. As children we were taught to play to win. If you don't win, there will be another game where you will have another chance to win. Somehow as adults, we lose this perspective. It is easy to internalize every defeat and setback into a constant negative stream of dialogue that your internal critic is more than willing to use against you if you allow it.

That dialogue might sound something like this:

- It's not my fault the boss likes him better than me.
- I'm not smart enough to figure out this project.
- If I ask for help, I'll look incompetent.
- Why didn't I get my degree?
- Why can't I lose twenty pounds?
- Life just isn't fair; everyone gets breaks but me.

Life becomes a stream of "what ifs" and regrets that interfere with your ability to move on and have the successful life you dream about. I know it may come as a surprise to some of you, but no one and no circumstance is holding you back but yourself. Let me say this again just for effect: You are the only person who can hold you back! You can either be controlled by your attitude or you can choose to have your attitude under control. Don't allow your attitude to defeat you. Don't listen to the negative comments and dire warnings, even from those closest to you, including you.

Someone who has their attitude under control knows that there are things they absolutely can't change. Bad things can and do happen to people every day. But these people have discovered that they can control how they respond to them. They choose to be optimistic and view problems as temporary issues. By doing this, they are able to focus on solutions rather than the problem.

In contrast, someone who does not have his or her attitude under control generally lacks faith in him or herself and has no idea how much power he or she truly possesses. When bad things happen, he or she tends to crumble under the weight of circumstance and becomes a victim until eventually his or her entire life is a series of seemingly insurmountable difficulties. He or she becomes convinced that the powers that be hate him or her, and he or she adopts a self-fulfilling fatalistic attitude. He or she allows their internal critic to tell them that it is no use trying to have a better life since they will fail anyway. By believing this and ceasing to try to improve themselves, he or she will soon doom him or herself to a life of pessimistic drudgery.

One of my favorite quotes is from *The Wizard of Oz*. When Glenda the Good Witch shows Dorothy that she can simply click her heels to return home, she says, "You had the power all along." This is true of most people today. They go through life searching for the elusive ideas of success and happiness, only to find that they existed within them the whole time. Once you understand that happiness and success are yours to create, you are ready to build a successful attitude.

Inside Out

In order to truly be happy, you must look inside yourself. The sad truth is that if you rely on happiness from external sources like your job, your family or your spouse, you will always be disappointed. They do not intentionally mean to hurt you, but these sources are people who are as imperfect as you are. If you focus on improving yourself and strive toward finding the joy within your own life, all of your relationships with other people will improve. They will notice your new attitude. They will see that you are no longer battered by circumstances as they are and will ask your secret.

Start Today

One of the wonderful things about being human is that we all have the ability to change ourselves. Many people have experienced the glory of a transformational epiphany that has redirected their entire lives. They stepped back and recognized the kind of power that exists in each one of us; then they set out to harness that power for themselves. That is what you are going to do. And it starts by reshaping your own attitude.

In order to do this, we have to understand where some of the negative attitudes and beliefs are coming from. This doesn't mean assigning blame. Our brains are programmed throughout our lives by things we are taught, experiences we have had, or people around us. Not all of the things that we learn or believe about ourselves are good. These form the basis of our internal dialogue.

Part of your internal dialogue may be that you aren't very smart, you aren't interested in the right things, or the things you do want are out of reach. There is an old saying that "misery loves company." Unfortunately, when one person in a particular group strives to achieve something beyond what he is used to, the reaction is negative rather than positive. We all live in a certain comfort zone, and if one of individuals within that zone steps up to a new level, the others try to pull him back. This is an interesting dichotomy unique to humans. We are social creatures and want to belong to a group. But if that group is holding you back, you must go forward even if it means losing some of those connections.

Our group mentality exists mostly out of fear: fear of failure, fear of the unknown, fear of loss. Though the people in your social or family circle may give you negative feedback, they will be convinced that they are saving you from disaster. Let's take a look back at my story. I was broke and had made a lot of mistakes financially. I took a risk when I decided to invest in real estate. I had very little money and now was going to invest in property. A few people in my life discouraged me by telling me I should save my money instead of throwing it away on the unknown. If we look back at this example, we recognize that the people in my life didn't discourage me due to lack of feeling. They discouraged me due to their own fears. They wanted me to stay where it was "safe." If I had listened to them I would still be staring into my empty bucket.

For many people, this sets up an attitude of helplessness. They think, "Damned if I do, damned if I don't." Some will spend their entire lives in this limbo, yearning for a better life but not having the courage to pursue it. They often become bitter and frustrated and have nothing to show for their lives but wasted dreams. Time is short, and dreams are to be grasped, not heaped onto a pile of regrets.

Positive Ideas

The first step to getting rid of an attitude of helplessness is to clear your mind of the negative dialogue from your internal critic. As you have a negative thought, stop your mind and replace the thought with a positive one. Negative thoughts build upon one another over time and crush your spirit. This could lead to bouts of depression and self-pity.

"Human beings, by changing the inner attitude of their minds, can change the outer aspect of their lives."
William James

Begin at the Beginning

So what would cause you to have a habitual bad attitude? Why would you live in constant fear, raining on other people's parades, and choose not to live an abundant and happy life? There are many possibilities, but most causes stem from past experiences and events in your life. Let's look at a few possibilities.

Inability to Release Past Hurts

Having a conflict with a family member or coworker can give you an attitude of resentment and anger. Do you feel that anger resurface every time you see this person? Do you lie awake at night thinking about the conflict? Do you wish the person harm? If so, then you have not let go of the conflict. This causes an attitude that hurts you more than anyone else and can poison your current relationships.

Low Self-Esteem

Do you avoid taking on new responsibilities so you won't risk failure? Do you put others down rather than congratulate their accomplishments? Do you refuse to assist coworkers for fear they may be after your job? If you find yourself with this kind of attitude, it may stem from having low self-esteem. You just don't believe in yourself or your abilities. Individuals with low self-esteem usually try to protect what they have rather than believing they can have more. The problem is that this negative attitude actually has the opposite effect. By refusing to help others and move forward, you may become the least-needed member of the group.

Fear

Fear is a natural emotion that protects us from danger. The problem is that many people imagine danger that does not exist or is minimal, and then they project that fear to be larger than life. This is paralyzing. A person living in fear will refuse to consider doing anything out of his idea of what is possible. He would rather not try at all than have something bad happen, like failure. These people also project their own fears onto those around them, encircling everyone they know with negative energy. They can't handle any type of change without feeling threatened or having an overall sense of impending doom.

Stress

This is a big one. Everyone feels stress on occasion, and no one is immune. The problem comes when that stress is allowed to build day after day, week after week, until it affects every part of your daily life. Stress will make you short-tempered, give you stomach problems, interfere with your ability to sleep, and may even give you thoughts of suicide just to escape the relentless pressure. Stress can give you a very negative attitude. Alleviating the stress in your life takes effort. After all, it didn't build up overnight, and it will take you days or weeks to figure out how to lessen the pressure and then more time to put your plan into action. You do have the power to change all of these problems in your life, but you must develop effective habits. You have to sit down and first figure out what needs changing and then write down possible solutions.

Monitoring your Attitude

One of the most important steps you can take in developing a new and successful attitude is to recognize when you are falling into a negative attitude. Self-awareness is a skill that can be learned by anyone. By being consciously aware of what kind of attitude you are projecting, you can ask yourself hard questions and determine where that attitude is coming from and how to stop it.

For example, do you ever get angry in traffic? Who hasn't, right? But think about it. Is being angry going to get you there faster? No. Is the anger going to affect the rest of your morning or even the whole day? Probably. Practice letting the emotion go. Listen to great music or buy a book you love on CD to focus on while you drive, and let the emotion go. Remind yourself that the negative energy doesn't affect the drivers in the other vehicles. It only hurts you. So let it go.

Once you get in the habit of examining your own attitude in daily situations, you will also begin to notice others' attitudes. People naturally want to be with those who have a positive outlook. Notice how these positive people go through their day and how others respond to a good attitude. This is what you want to achieve.

So the question is, are you a positive person? Do you see the glass as half-full or half-empty? Answering the questions in the quiz below will help you to determine your outlook on life.

1. You didn't stick to your diet today. You ate a piece of candy.

   a) Who cares? Your friends and family love you for you, not your weight.

b) You forgive yourself for this little mistake and work harder tomorrow.

c) You should have known. You can't lose weight by eating candy.

d) You think that you have failed miserably and give up on your diet completely. You go back to your old eating habits.

2. Your computer crashes and you just lost all of your data.

a) You pull out your backup drive and begin to rewrite your proposal. You would have had to do a few rewrites anyway, so now it will be even better.

b) You breathe a few deep breaths and call the computer helpline for your company.

c) You worry that you may not have backed up all of your files.

d) You yell and scream at the screen and then punch the keyboard with your fists.

3. Your boss just gave you the biggest account in the company.

a) You thank him and look at this as an opportunity for advancement.

b) You ask your coworkers for help because you want to give this account and your client the best possible service.

c) You decline the project because you've heard through the water cooler gossip that this client is demanding and hard to work with.

d) You quit on the spot. You don't think that you are capable of this type of responsibility.

4. You've decided to buy the car of your dreams. When the salesman asks you if you want to buy the extended warranty, you say:

    a) Of course, you never know when it will come in handy.
    b) I don't want to spend the extra money, but I know that accidents happen.
    c) The warranty only covers 30,000 miles. Don't you have one that covers more miles?
    d) You car salesmen are always out to make a buck. These warranties aren't as good as the paper they are printed on.

5. Your child brings home an F on her progress report.

    a) You call and talk to the teacher to verify the grade and ask how you can help the situation.
    b) You devise a plan to review homework together every night to raise the grade.
    c) You punish the child and hire a tutor.
    d) You stop saving for college and take the dream vacation you never could afford. If your child can't pass a class, she obviously isn't going to go to college.

6. You wake up feeling like you have the flu.

    a) You think that you must have slept wrong, and it will go away before morning's end.
    b) You take some aspirin and get ready for the day.
    c) You go straight to the hospital because you think you have a terrible disease.
    d) You call your lawyer to make an appointment to get your affairs in order.

7. You've heard all over town that the newest
restaurant has the best food, but it didn't get good reviews from
the local newspaper.

     a) You can't wait to go. Your own opinion has more
          value than others.

     b) You go with the attitude that if it isn't very good
          food, at least you got a night out on the town.

     c) Don't worry about it. Restaurants charge too much
          for mediocre food anyway.

     d) You hate it because the newspaper hates it. You
          don't even bother wasting your time.

8. Your new puppy had an accident on your carpet this morning,
this afternoon and this evening. And as you are answering this
quiz, you notice he has done it again.

     a) That's okay. You can clean it up. After all he is just a
         puppy. He'll learn soon enough.

     b) You enroll him in doggy training.

     c) You toss him on the patio. He is now an outside
         dog.

     d) You find a farm for him to live on.

9. You just heard that you might be laid off due to budget cuts.

     a) You work overtime and take on more assignments.
         If they can see your value, they might keep you.

     b) You continue to do a good job but start to send a
         few "feelers" out about potential jobs.

     c) You arrive to work an hour late, take a long lunch
         and leave early. Why work hard for a company that
         wants to put you out of a job?

d) You round up boxes for your personal items. You are out of here. You don't really deserve the big salary and corner office.

- Score your answers. Did any of those scenarios sound familiar? Let's see what that answers mean:
- Mostly A's. You go through life wearing rose-colored glasses. Be careful. You could be glossing over issues instead of dealing with them. This could cause you big trouble in the future.
- Mostly B's. You have a great outlook on life. Your positive thinking has helped you to have an abundant life. You are the type of person that people want to be around and strive to be like. Congratulations!
- Mostly C's. You are a bit on the pessimistic side. It is good to be cautious, but don't let it keep you from accomplishing any future successes.
- Mostly D's. You expect the worst from every situation. Odds are that you are very unhappy. Living your life with a catastrophic view wears not only on you, but also those around you too.

How did you rate? No matter your score, you can always change your attitude. Remember, your habits are a huge determining factor of your outcome in life.

"You are the only person on earth who can use your ability."

Zig Ziglar

Chapter Four

Transforming Your Mind

Chapter Four

Transforming Your Mind

No one sets out in life to fail. Our nature strives for more, desires more, and dreams of all the possibilities the future holds. If you ask any five-year-old, she can articulate a list of dreams she already has for her life, which might include her future occupation, but will almost always include how she will feel. She wants to be happy.

As we all grow into adulthood, our idea of financial freedom takes the form of specific habits. We want an education, a good job, and a family. Most people work very hard to achieve these things, and many attain them but remain unhappy. Until you are able to form productive habits, your finances will be out of balance. In order to change your life, you have to make the decision to change your habits. The ability to live the life of your dreams is not being withheld from you by any person or any obstacle. No one stands in your way – no one but you.

"The state of your life is nothing more than a reflection of your state of mind."

Wayne Dyer

Habits for many people are powerful and, for most, intimately entwined with their lives. They want freedom from work, bills and the daily grind of living a life that is not exactly what they imagined. However, they have no idea how to go about setting into motion a process to change and rebalance their finances. Feeling trapped, they move through each day doing the same things, accepting their fate and giving in to emotional helplessness.

Imagine how your life would look and what you would do differently if you changed your bad habits. Would you be working as much or even have the same job? Would you still work for others, building their dreams, or would you start your own business? Would you share more of your life with family and friends? Would you travel and see the world?

Understand that this exercise is not about quitting your job. This is about changing your habits to live a lifestyle that gives you what you want. If you love your current job, then you only need to expand your lifestyle to achieve more balance and look for other opportunities that enhance your existing skills.

You don't have to be CEO to achieve a lifestyle of abundance. You can be anything. By starting with what you have and where you are right now in your life, you can change your habits and accomplish great things.

The Mindset of Financial Freedom

Each person has an idea of what the perfect life would be. For some this may be living in a certain location or type of home. Others may want more time to spend with children, parents and friends. Some may also view it as the opportunity to share with others or build a business. Think about what your perfect lifestyle would be. Much of your life depends on your habits, so the formation of good habits is important to bring about the life of your dreams.

But old habits, like thinking small, are hard to break. We all can get caught up in the mindset of lack, but the difference between you and people who realize their dreams is not in what they have or how they live. It is in their habits. The have fostered a mindset of habits. They think in a certain way, and this enables them to bring abundance into their lives through effective habits.

Some of our habits are so ingrained that we don't even realize we do them, yet they have a tremendous impact on our lives. The mindset of habits acknowledges that we can accomplish anything we want. Once you understand that there is no limit to your life, you will revel in life's abundance.

Many of us know what to do. We want to live abundantly with our time as our own. We know we should look for opportunities, take the most promising ones and move forward. We want different results in our lives, so we focus on change. The problem is that we do not change our habits. We focus on the negative. It is important to understand that "that which you think about, you become." It is a conscious decision to accept the mindset of habit, and it takes effort.

This applies to all areas of your life in which you wish to experience abundance, whether it is family, health, or finances. Think for a moment of all the detrimental health habits people have. Some smoke, drink to excess or refuse to exercise. It is no secret that these choices are bad for people's health, yet many refuse to change. They cling strongly to those habits and associate with those who have similar habits, further validating their poor choices. The power to change any aspect of your life is completely within your control, but only if you change your thoughts. This could also mean changing your associations, but it is necessary if you truly want to live an abundant life. In order to transform your habits, you must first transform the mind.

When we take away group habits, what we call culture, we are all essentially alike. We need and want a balanced lifestyle to feel happy, healthy and have a high quality of life. It doesn't matter that we speak different languages, have different beliefs or pursue different goals. Our minds still work in exactly the same fashion. We all have intellectual skills that make us completely different than any other animal, yet we posses these same skills across all cultures and races. They are uniquely human.

We are all born with five senses: sight, taste, touch, hearing and smell. By the age of five, most children have a complete understanding of their ability to use their five senses to understand the world and environment around them. The five senses are limited to telling us and showing us what already "is." They have no power to create or transform.

Intellectual skills do have the power to create and transform your habits. They are present in each one of us, and each identifies a powerful area of thought that we can use to change our habits and transform our lives.

The six intellectual skills are:
* Reasoning
* Intuition
* Perception
* Will
* Imagination
* Memory

In order for us to utilize our mind to alter our habits, we must exercise these skills, which are much like mental muscles. It is also important to understand that these skills are always at work. However, they may be weak or strong depending on how much you use them, just like your muscles. Your ability to have the life of your dreams starts with your habits. Being able to form productive habits is proportional to the development, integration and strength of these six faculties which expand infinitely when exercised. Let's take a closer look at each one.

Reasoning

Reasoning is our ability to make sense of events in our world. Deductive reasoning is our default thought process that ensures that we will continue to be a product of our environment. Deductive reasoning relies on your current understanding and conditioning at the subconscious level for guidance.

When you are using deductive reasoning, you will quickly reject anything that doesn't match your current understanding or paradigms. This guarantees that you will continue to act on ideas that keep that paradigm in place, and you are likely to reject an idea that would move your life or wealth forward. You will also likely stay in your comfort zone when you are being deductive, and your attitudes will be created by your surrounding environment rather than creating the environment that surrounds you. You are purely deductive when your environment creates you, and you are being inductive when you create your own environment. Inductive reasoning (true thinking) occurs when we use our intuition, perception, will, imagination and memory to analyze new ideas and then create and support the picture of what we want to see in our lives.

Intuition

Often referred to as our "sixth sense," intuition is our ability to connect with another individual without even knowing or speaking to him. When we meet someone who immediately makes us feel good or positive, that person projects a positive energy and our intuition senses it. When we meet someone who makes us feel negative or scared, our intuition immediately warns us of the negativity.

Napoleon Hill's *Think and Grow Rich* explains that when you demand a definite plan from your mind for abundance, you must be on alert because it will and must answer you; but it will do so through *inspired thought,* or the sixth sense. When the still small voice answers, you must act immediately. Failure to do so will be fatal to success. Developing your intuition to tune in to the highest level of those around you allows you to see through all the noise of conversation and immediately understand the essence of who they are and what they are about.

Perception

This is what we use to create meaning from events or experiences in our lives. We interpret these based on past events and conditioning. An important concept to understand with perception is that everything is relative. Nothing has meaning or is good or bad until we make it so. Thus, each person will have a different perception or interpretation of exactly the same event or object.

It would be a mistake to underestimate the role of perception in our daily lives. It has the power to alter our attitude and course of direction almost without our notice. It takes much strength of will to change perceptions we have held for a long time.

Will

This is our ability to hold an image, idea or thought that we want in our conscious mind until it has the chance to embed itself into our subconscious so that the idea can manifest itself in our lives. It is much like a lens we can adjust and focus. The will allows us to take any subconscious idea that may have been present in our minds since childhood and change it. We do this by intense concentration over time and with repetition. Any habit that we want to stop or change encounters our will. The term "will power" has been used in conjunction with weight loss, tobacco use and exercise, but it can also be used to stop habitual thoughts or negative self-doubt.

Imagination

This is our creative power. We have the ability to create airplanes, fax machines, the Internet, automobiles and light bulbs against all doubt and odds because of the power of imagination combined with the other intellectual skills. Your imagination is either imagining how you can do something or why you can't.

Napoleon Hill tells us that we have Creative Imagination and Synthetic Imagination. Creative Imagination is what works with the infinite intelligence to bring forth a new plan previously unaware to us at the conscious level, whereas Synthetic Imagination is where we use our current pool of knowledge and resources to create. Hill also called our imagination the "workshop of the mind." Inside this workshop we need to use and develop our skills for both our Creative and Synthetic Imaginations if we are to produce the results we desire.

Memory

This is our ability to recall previous events and experiences. Many of us tend to remember only our failures, and those memories seem to linger much longer and be more intense than our memories of success. Rather, we should use our memory to bolster our confidence and self-esteem as we try something new. At some point, everything was new to us, yet we learned. We must exercise our memory to work in our favor and remind us that we can do anything we set our mind to. By consciously focusing on past successes, no matter how small, our overall self-confidence is improved. Every person reading this book has succeeded at multiple things in life to get to this point.

Claim those successes and remember them every time you set your course for a new journey in life.

Competitive Plane vs. Creative Plane

How do you envision your bucket being filled? Do you think about making as much money as fast as you can? Do you search only for "ground floor" opportunities because all of the good ones are exhausted? Do you want to hurry and take as much as you can while the "getting is good?" Or do you want to fill your bucket with as much as you need because you know that there will always be more available?

If you answered "yes" to the first few questions, you are living on the Competitive Plane. You take as much as you can because the universe has limited resources. Your actions dictate your outcomes. If you act in such a manner, you are projecting lack, which is what you will receive in return. If you answered "yes" to the last question, however, you are living on the creative plane. You take as much as you need because the universe has an inexhaustible supply of resources.

The universe will make all of its resources available for you. You do not need to take things away from someone else. It is imperative for you to rid your mind of the concept of competition. The universe intends for you to create, not to compete for what is already created.

When you go into the world to fill your bucket, remember the following:

- There is no need to take anything away from anyone.
- You are to become a creator, not a competitor; you will

get what you want, but in such a way that when you get it, every other person in the universe will have more than they have now.

- You do not have to take advantage of anyone.
- No one has anything that you can't have. There is enough for everyone.

Wealth secured on the competitive plane is never satisfactory or permanent and won't lead you to financial freedom. It is here today and gone tomorrow. Remember, in order for you to obtain true financial freedom, you must shift your mindset from competitive to creative. Never allow yourself to think for a moment that the universal supply is limited. You have returned to the competitive mind the moment you start to believe that you have to go against the natural flow of the universe in order for you to fill your bucket. As a result, you've left your higher state of conscious awareness, which reverses any financial freedom that you may have already earned.

Train your mind to always look at the limitless supply; push away any thought of the visible supply. Impress upon your conscious awareness that financial freedom is coming to you as fast as you can receive it. Nobody can prevent you from obtaining unlimited wealth. For example, if you are planning to buy a ranch in the mountains, don't allow yourself to think that all of the scenic real estate will be gone. That will cause you to make a decision in haste. Losing what you want to someone else is impossible because you are not seeking anything that is possessed by anybody else. You are causing what you want to be created from the universe's limitless supply.

Once you accept the truth that on the creative plane, as opposed to the competitive plane, there can never be a lack of opportunity, you will immediately begin to live a life driven by financial freedom.

"We make our habits, and then our habits make us."

John Dryden

Chapter Five

Invest in Yourself

Chapter Five

Invest in Yourself

A habit is defined as an action done often and easily. Our lives are made up of all kinds of habits. Almost everything we do involves the use of habitual behavior. Stop and think about it. You get up in the morning and use habits to get ready to start the day. Otherwise, you would have to relearn everything you do – combing your hair, brushing your teeth, dressing, working the toaster and even pouring a glass of milk.

"If you create an act, you create a habit. If you create a habit, you create a character. If you create a character, you create a destiny."

Andre Maurois

How do we go about changing a habit? You just do it differently. Sound simple enough? You get up the next day and do it differently again. And the next day you get up and stop doing it again. Try doing just one thing different in your morning routine. If you usually eat breakfast before taking a shower, take a shower first and then eat breakfast. Then practice your new habit every morning.

Daily habits might not be too hard, but what about those habitual behaviors that prevent you from taking control of your financial future? The habits you have learned from your limiting behaviors, the things you do that are self-defeating, are the habits that are hard to change.

Habits are done frequently and automatically and are difficult to stop. Most people think of behaviors when they think of habits, but thoughts can also become habits. Sometimes our habitual thinking can keep habitual behaviors going and make them hard to change. All too often, we fall prey to our habits because we agree with the sabotaging thoughts that the voice in our head proposes.

Bad Habits versus. Good Habits

Habits can be good or bad. Good habits help us get through our daily lives. When we go to work in the morning, we use a number of habits. Likewise, stopping at red lights, looking both ways before crossing a street and slowing down at busy intersections are all good habits that protect us. Of course, we can also develop some pretty bad habits, ones that can be harmful to us and to other people. For example, we could get into the habit of failing to pay attention to our surroundings once they become familiar.

So, how do we know if a habit is a good one, a bad one, or neither good nor bad? Many of us go through life on autopilot, not actually realizing that our actions are forming bad habits.

We are often unaware that this behavior is dictating our future. Before we know it, we are caught in an all-consuming, seemingly never-ending cycle of negative behavior and bad habits. Ask yourself if you are engaging in any of the following detrimental bad habits:

- Think, Say, and Do Negative Things. You see problems in every opportunity. You are a habitual complainer. No matter what it is, you will complain about it. The rain ruined your picnic. Your coffee is too hot. You think that everyone you meet has an agenda and is out to get you. You always look for problems, never for solutions. Every little bit of difficulty is exaggerated to the point of tragedy. All failures, no matter how small, are catastrophes. You get discouraged easily and don't view mistakes as tools for learning. You are stuck in life but can't move forward because you are too afraid to move out of your comfort zone.

- Act Before You Think. Your actions are based on instinct or impulse. If you see something you want, you buy it at once without any second thought. Then you may see something better and regret not taking the time to comparison shop for the best bargain. You don't think about the future. Your only concern is immediate pleasure. Consequences are of no concern to you. Your ultimate goal is to get what you want right now, no matter what the outcome.

- Talk Instead of Listening. You want to be the center of attention. So you always engage in boastful conversations even to the point of not being truthful. Most of the time, no one understands what you are talking about. You never listen to advice. You are too proud to admit your mistakes and will often repeat them just to prove a point. In your mind you are always right and reject any suggestions because that will make you feel inferior.

- Call it Quits. Successful people treat failures as stepping stones to success. You call it quits as soon as you recognize the first signs of failure. At first, you may be excited to start a project, but then you lose interest fairly quickly, especially when you encounter problems. You don't have the persistence to fulfill your dreams. You should never quit because you never know how close you are to achieving your goals.

- Bring Those Around You Down. You envy other successful people. Rather than working hard yourself, you spread rumors and try to bring them down. Instead of asking successful people for advice and guidance, you would rather wallow in your own misfortune because of pride. You vibrate negativity into the universe, which only returns back to you.

- Poor Time Management. You don't know how to plan your schedule. You waste time watching TV or daydreaming about what you want your life to be like, instead of actually planning for it. You fill your mind with useless fantasies of improving your life, instead of making an actual plan. Time should be managed efficiently in order to succeed.

- Take the Easy Road. You don't want to experience any suffering or hardship. You want a good life without any trials or sacrifices. Successful people make it through trial and error. They never give up. They are willing to do everything necessary to achieve their aspirations in life.

Positive habits can be very powerful in your life, as well as can bad habits. Positive habits are great because they can automatically help you to accomplish your goals in life and make you wealthier. That is the greatest quality of positive habits; they are automatic. You don't have to think about them, and they lead your life in the direction you want to go. The opposite effect can happen for bad habits. They automatically take you in the direction you don't want to go. Fortunately, the steps to forming and breaking bad habits are simple, but that doesn't make them easy to do.

"Great is the power of habit. It teaches us to bear fatigue and to despise wounds and pain."
Marcus Tullius Cicero

Most experts think it takes twenty-one days to form or break a habit. If you have the self-discipline to halt a bad habit for twenty-one days, you will be able to change your ways. Another factor when considering habit formation is your emotional intensity tied to that habit. For example, many people eat because of how it makes them feel. Some people believe that they need to eat to relax; they believe it with their whole heart. For this person, breaking the bad habit of over-eating is going to be much harder due to the emotional attachment to eating. You should harness the power of positive habits to take your life where you want to go and automatically accomplish your goals. You can start with this easy plan: Keep track of your habits. Write down every time you engage in your habit. What are you doing when your habit surfaces? What are you thinking? How are you feeling? List the pros and cons of keeping your habit and the advantages of changing.

Why Habits Are Difficult to Change

Desire is a major factor to consider when you are analyzing your ability to change a bad habit into a good one. The stronger the desire, the faster the change will occur. A person who comes face to face with serious health consequences if he doesn't give up smoking is highly motivated. With the desire to live, he can overcome a lack of self-discipline and change the habit. What we may think of as poor self-discipline might just be a lack of real desire. We can tap into tremendous reserves to change our habits just by getting in touch with the power of our authentic desire.

Conflicting desires are a large reason that people fail to make habit changes in their lives. They may claim a lack self-discipline or personal power, but they don't notice the effects of conflicting desires on their habitual choices. Let's suppose that someone wants to give up unhealthy foods, but keeps finding it too tempting to pass up dessert or give up those potato chips as a snack. The desire for the pleasure associated with the snack competes with the intent to eat healthy.

These conflicting desires can zap our energy, but there is another challenge that causes us to continue our bad eating habits. It happens after we have the dessert or eat the potato chips. If we fall to the temptation of that piece of cheesecake, the damage doesn't usually end there. The negative inner voice in our head chimes in with condemnations about our choice. It puts us down, tells us we failed and works to convince us that we don't have the self-discipline and personal will-power to stop the unhealthy eating habit.

If we agree with the voice, our mind effectively hypnotizes us into the continuation of our bad habits. We use our will-power to invest in the belief that we have no self-discipline to change. This type of self-hypnosis can be more damaging to our emotional well-being than any amount of food we eat. The problem for many people isn't that they lack self-discipline to change. It is that they have already invested it in agreements about being powerless.

Awareness

You don't have to be powerless against your finances. You do have the power to change your habits. All you need to do is substitute a behavior for your habit. It needs to be incompatible with your habit, something you can't do while engaging in your habit.

The first part of changing a habit is awareness training. What are you thinking, doing and feeling when your habit shows up? Who are you with? These are habit-prone situations. Sometimes we can try to stay away from these situations or places, but often they are with us every day. Indeed, you can avoid the temptation to do certain activities by staying away from certain places and people and changing your behavior.

The behavior needs to be something you can do for as long as you have the urge to engage in your habit. It also needs to be something that will be convenient and something you can do in public without being noticed. If you often engage in your habit while participating in other activities, your new behavior will need to be something that will not interfere with these other activities.

Your new behavior will not only help keep you from engaging in your habit, it will also help you become more aware of what you are doing or not doing. Habits are often automatic. We do them without thinking about what we are doing. This added awareness helps the behavior become less automatic. Let's try a simple exercise for substituting a behavior for a habit.

Substitution Exercise

List several behaviors that could prevent you from performing your bad habit. List all the behaviors that come to mind. When you can't think of another behavior, stop and examine your list. Pick out the ones that meet the criteria we set forth above. The behavior must be something that:

- You can do for an unlimited amount of time.
- Is convenient for you in any situation.
- Is able to be performed in any location.
- Won't interfere with your or anyone else's other activities.

Now, narrow down your list; then pick a behavior to help you to change your habit. Don't worry about it being the perfect behavior. If this one doesn't work, you can choose another behavior. You might want to have two or three possible ones. For example, if overeating or excessive snacking is a problem, you could let yourself choose from reading, needlework and walks outdoors.

After you've picked one or more good behaviors, take a few moments to list the pros and cons of engaging in this behavior instead of your habit. Hopefully, the advantages will outweigh the disadvantages, just as the disadvantages of your habit outweighed the advantages. If not, you may want to choose another behavior.

Reward yourself for even small successes. Have a pre-planned self-reward system in place to reinforce your new behaviors. If your new plan includes continuing to spend a certain amount of money on your wardrobe, but limiting yourself to only one new outfit a week, give yourself a pat on the back each time you succeed. Eventually, this new behavior will be routine, but in the early stages it should be reinforced.

So what can you do with these times and situations when the urge to engage in your habit can be overwhelming? Increase your awareness at these times. We need to be extra alert when our habit is likely to show up because the urge could seem almost overwhelming. Be creative. Take a look at the notes that you've kept on your habit. How can you alter your environment to reduce the urge to engage in your habit? What situations, places and people could you avoid while you're working on your habit? When do you need to be extra alert?

Successful habit change takes action. But action isn't enough. To succeed you'll need commitment. It's time to take action and make that habit change you've thought about and planned for so long. When you're ready for change, nothing feels as good as actively doing something to positively affect your life. You're committed. If you've properly planned for this change, your commitment to the new you should be very strong. You can visualize how your new life will be. This commitment will assure your long-term success.

"Vision without action is a dream. Action without vision is simply passing the time. Action with Vision is making a positive difference."

Joel Barker

Chapter Six

Envisioning Your Life

Chapter Six

Envisioning Your Life

Vision is the manner in which one sees or conceives of something. It is a mental image produced by your imagination. Also, vision is a person or thing of extraordinary beauty. Success on any major scale requires a clear vision and consistent action. Your life is a direct result of your dominant thoughts. Nothing happens by itself. It all comes your way once you have a clear vision and consistent thinking and action based on your vision.

Creating a vision for your life is imperative for you to succeed on your personal journey to financial success. The process of creating your vision will allow you to plan where you want to go in life. In order for you to achieve your life's dreams, you must first concentrate your efforts on a strategic plan. First, you need to decide what you want to accomplish in your life. You do this by writing down your life's vision. This lifetime vision will lay the foundation for all of your future decisions. Try to balance your lifetime vision with all important areas of your life. Consider the following areas:

- Education. What do you need to know in order to achieve your vision?
- Career. How successful do you want to be? Do you want to be executive management?
- Financial. How much money do you want to have by a certain age?
- Family. Do you and your partner have the same vision? Do you both want children?
- Physical. Do you want to live a healthy life so that you can enjoy your wealth and success? How will you ensure that you live a long, healthy life?
- Attitude. What is holding you back?
- Satisfaction. Are you satisfied with your life? What vision will help you to improve your satisfaction?
- Positive Existence. How will your vision enable you to become a productive member of society and thus vibrate throughout the universe, making it a better place?

After you define your life's vision, review it to ensure that you are absolutely satisfied that it reflects what you want your life to be. It is important to note that your vision should be your own, not your spouse's, parents' or employers.' Don't let any anyone or anything influence your life's vision.

"Vision is the gift of seeing clearly what may be. Vision expands our horizons. The more we see, the more we can achieve; the grander our vision, the more glorious our accomplishment."

Unknown

Once you have set your life's vision, you've paved the road to a life filled with abundance and fulfillment. This vision may seem like a big undertaking at first. Don't let it overwhelm you. First, you must remember that this is your life's vision. So it probably won't be accomplished overnight. That's okay. You need to set a plan for achieving this vision. For example, this could be a twenty-five or thirty year plan. Divide this plan into stages such as a ten years, five years and one year.

Visionary Boards

The Law of Attraction is simply the universal law that we attract into our lives those things we hold in our minds. A very powerful way to achieve success by using the Law of Attraction is by creating a visionary board. It is one of the most powerful ways to make the Law of Attraction work for you. A visionary board is a picture collage of the goals and dreams you want to attract in your life. It is very important to use the exact image of what you want to attract, as whatever you have on your visionary board will become part of your reality!

Choose the thoughts and actions that will lead to your vision. Nobody can do it for you. Only you can make it happen when your vision is clear. You're the only one with the power to live your vision. Once you have a visionary board, you have the power to succeed at anything. The power to fulfill your dreams starts with the ability to represent your vision on the board.

For several years I used the visionary board technique to analyze and make complex decisions regarding my financial situation. Visionary boards can help you to develop a concentrated and inquisitive mind. You must practice your mental concentration and visualization daily to master the use of visionary boards. The most difficult part of a visionary board is learning how to relax your mind and body. If you already know how to relax, you are fifty percent ahead of the game.

Understanding your mind and body at the deepest level and making the mental and physical changes are crucial for managing your emotional and intellectual state. This is necessary for learning how to relax and grow personally. By doing this and practicing with visionary boards, you can grow and achieve everything you want.

Visionary boards are simple and will help you achieve anything you desire in life. You can use visionary boards and learn to think like the greatest minds in history. With daily practice of visionary boards, you will be able to unleash the *power of your creative mind and better manage your finances.*

"Our intention creates our reality. Anything you really want, you can attain, if you really go after it."
Wayne Dyer

Visionary boards put your desires into your mind and bring them to your attention. Whatever you put your attention on increases. Whatever you remove your attention from vanishes. Visionary boards are the best tools for effectively paying attention to your intentions.

How to Use Visionary Boards

To be truly successful and confident in life, you must map your mind and make things obvious and understandable to other people. I can accomplish anything I want, thanks to discipline and the visionary board I use to educate my mind. This method is a simple way to apply pictures, words, arrows and signs in analyzing, learning, understanding and remembering new concepts. Visionary boards are so simple that elementary school children can learn the concept in five minutes. A few suggestions on how to use visionary boards include the following:

- Make your visionary board a habit. This board is to be lived, not just read. Use your visionary board to create a mental map of what you want in life and make it a part of your daily life. Look at it every day. Hang it up in a commonly frequented area of your house so you will see it every day. A constant reminder of your vision in life will open your mind to creative thinking.

- Live your passion. You will never achieve real success unless you find and live your passion. Your chances for success will be directly proportional to the degree of pleasure you derive from what you do. If you have a job you hate, face the fact squarely and get out. Work must be rewarding, not a form of punishment.

- Make your thoughts real. Creating the blueprints for your success is the first step to making your thoughts real. Journaling your thoughts will help you graphically represent your thinking and will greatly enhance your mental and muscle memory. Also, there is something about putting your thoughts in writing that makes them seem more real.

- Expect success. Life is largely a matter of expectation. You must expect success if you want to succeed. When you expect things to happen, strangely enough, they do happen. Expectation energizes your visions, giving them momentum. When you consistently expect something good to happen, it will happen. The dreams you believe in become a reality.

- Set your expectations high, even if they appear to be unrealistic. If you begin with a wild expectation, you'll succeed beyond your wildest expectations. Applying visionary boards to your expectations will help you succeed at anything in life.

"The only limits in our life are those we impose on ourselves."

Bob Proctor

Combining visionary boards with positive affirmations will enable you to accomplish any goal you put your mind to. So, how do you use positive affirmations? The method you use strongly influences their effectiveness. Below are some guidelines for using positive affirmations:

- Make positive statements. When you talk about your goals, use positive expressions. Say phrases like, "I can do this" instead of, "Don't be stupid and mess up."
- Give your affirmations precise dates, times and amounts so you can measure your achievements and success.
- Prioritize your affirmations. Give each of them a priority. This practice helps you to avoid feeling overwhelmed by too many and helps to direct your attention to the most important ones.
- Write all of your affirmations down. This will help to reinforce them in your mind.

"My will shall shape the future. Whether I fail or succeed shall be no man's doing but my own. I am the force; I can clear any obstacle before me or I can be lost in the maze. My choice; my responsibility; win or lose, only I hold the key to my destiny."
Elaine Maxwell

Take Action Now

Take action now by creating a visionary board. It is a simple project. All you need is a poster board, scissors, glue and tons of magazines. Go through the magazines and search for images of your dreams or search for the right images on the internet. Cut out the images and glue them on your poster board. For more power, add affirmations such as, "I love living in my 10,000 square feet house" or, "I love earning a million dollars per year." This reinforces what you desire.

Hang your poster board on a spot where you will see it regularly, such as at your desk or in the kitchen. Look at it daily and really believe that you have already achieved the things on your visionary board. Look at your board as often as possible with focused intent. You will be surprised to see the things on your visionary board appear in your life sooner or later, provided you keep putting your intention on them and stay positive. By looking at your visionary board daily, you will manifest the life you truly desire and deserve!

"If you dream it, you can achieve it. You will get all you want in life if you help enough other people get what they want."

Zig Ziglar

Chapter Seven

The Importance of Effective Time Management

Chapter Seven

The Importance of Effective Time Management

Many of us spend our lives in a frenzy of activity but achieve very little because we are not concentrating on the right things. One reason is because we only think of time as a set amount. True, we only have twenty-four hours in a given day. However, it is not the time that matters, but our perception of it. Hence, we don't know how to effectively manage time. These are essential skills for effective people.

People who routinely utilize their time effectively are the highest achievers in all walks of life, from business to sports to public services. If you use these skills well, you will be able to function effectively, even under intense pressure. For us to shift our mindset regarding time to work smarter and improve time utilization, we need to concentrate on results, not on being busy.

*"There are three constants in life . . .
change, choice and principles."*
Stephen Covey

Have you ever heard of "80:20 Rule?" This rule argues that typically eighty percent of unfocused effort generates only twenty percent of the results. The remaining eighty percent of the results are achieved with only twenty percent of the effort. By applying this rule to your life, you can optimize your effort to ensure that you concentrate as much of your time and energy as possible on the high priority tasks. This ensures that you achieve the greatest benefit possible with the limited amount of time available to you.

Procrastination

Do you put off important tasks over and over again? If your answer is "yes," you're not alone. In fact, a majority of people procrastinate to some degree, but for some, procrastination has become such a bad habit that it disrupts their life and prevents them from achieving the things they're capable of.

The key to controlling and ultimately combating this destructive habit is to recognize when you start procrastinating, understand why it happens and take active steps to better manage your time and outcomes.

The main reason most people procrastinate is they just don't want to do a certain activity. You put off things that you should be focusing on right now, usually in favor of doing something that is more enjoyable or that you're more comfortable doing. Procrastinators work as many hours in the day as other people, but they invest their time in the wrong tasks. Sometimes this is simply because they don't understand the difference between urgent tasks and important tasks and jump straight to the urgent tasks that aren't actually important.

Another common cause of procrastination is feeling overwhelmed. You may not know where to begin. Or you may not believe that you are capable or have the skills or resources you think you need. As a result, you seek comfort in doing tasks you know you're capable of completing. Unfortunately, the big task isn't going to go away. Truly important tasks rarely do. If you're putting off starting a project because you find it overwhelming, try to break the project into a set of smaller, more manageable tasks. Once you accomplish one small task, you'll start to feel that you're achieving things, and soon the whole project won't seem so overwhelming. Other causes of procrastination include these things:

- Waiting for the right time. There never is a right time. Just do it and move on to the next task.
- A fear of failure or success.
- Indecisiveness.
- Poor organizational skills.

Overcoming Procrastination

No matter your reason for procrastinating, you must control it before it becomes a habit. Once it becomes a habit, you miss opportunities, or your career is derailed. Use the following tools to help you to overcome procrastination:

- Recognition. If you're completely honest with yourself, you probably know when you're procrastinating. Make sure you know your priorities. Delaying an unimportant task may not necessarily be procrastination; it may just be good task prioritization.
- Find out why you're procrastinating. Why you procrastinate depends on both you and the task. But it's important to understand what the reasons for

procrastination are for each situation, so that you can select the best approach for overcoming your reluctance to get going.

- Motivate yourself. If you are putting something off because you just don't want to do it, you need to find ways of motivating yourself to get moving.

Create an Activity Journal

How long do you spend each day on unimportant things, things that don't really contribute to your success at work? Do you know how much time you've spent reading junk mail, talking to colleagues, making coffee and eating lunch? And how often have you thought, "I could achieve so much more if I just had another hour each day."

Are you aware of when you check your e-mail, write important articles, or do your long-term planning? Most people find they function at different levels of effectiveness at different times of day as their energy levels fluctuate. Your effectiveness may vary depending on the amount of breakfast you ate, the length of time since you last took a break, distractions, stress and discomfort.

Activity journals help you analyze how you actually spend your time. The first time you use an activity journal, you won't believe the amount of time you waste on any given day. You'll find that your memory is a very poor guide when it comes to remembering how you spent your time.

Keeping an activity journal for several days helps you to understand how you spend your time and when you perform at your best. Without modifying your behavior any further than you have to, write down the things you do. Every time you change activities, whether reading e-mail, working, cooking or talking on the phone, write down the time of the change.

As well as recording your activities, write down how you feel: alert, tired, energetic, etc. Do this periodically throughout the day. You may decide to integrate your activity journal with a stress diary. Once you have recorded your activities for a few days, analyze your journal. You will be able to track the amount of time you spend doing unimportant tasks. Also, you will be able to see your energy levels during different parts of the day. With this information at hand, you should be able to determine where you can free up extra time in your day by applying one of the following actions to most activities.

Action Lists

Do you feel overwhelmed by the amount of work you have to do? Do you face a constant barrage of looming deadlines? Do you sometimes just forget to do something important so that people have to chase you to get work done?

All of these are symptoms of not keeping an action list. Action lists are prioritized lists of all the tasks that you need to carry out. They list everything that you have to do, with the most important tasks at the top of the list and the least important tasks at the bottom. Starting to keep a list effectively is often the first personal productivity and time management breakthrough that people make as they start to make a success of their careers.

By keeping an action list, you make sure that you record all of the tasks you have to complete in one place. This is essential if you're not going to forget things. And by prioritizing tasks, you plan the order in which you need to do activities, so you can tell what needs your immediate attention and what you can set aside until later.

Action lists are very simple and extremely powerful, both as a method of organizing yourself and as a way of reducing stress. Often problems may seem overwhelming, or you may have a seemingly huge number of demands on your time. This may leave you feeling out of control and overburdened with work.

"The supreme value is not the future but the present. The future is a deceitful time that always says to us, 'Not yet,' and thus denies us. The future is not the time of love; what man truly wants he wants now. Whoever builds a house for future happiness builds a prison for the present."

Octavio Paz

Preparing an Action List

First, write down your tasks for the day, month, quarter and year, whatever suits you best. If they are large, break them down into smaller tasks. If these still seem large, break them down again. Do this until you have listed everything that you have to do and until the tasks listed will take no more than a couple of hours to complete.

Once you have done this, prioritize your tasks. If too many tasks have a high priority, read through the list again and demote the less important ones. Once you have done this, rewrite the list in priority order. You will then have a precise plan that you can use to eliminate problems. You will be able to tackle these in order of importance. This allows you to separate important tasks from the many time-consuming trivial ones.

Effective Scheduling

Plan your time. Make time for yourself. So far we have looked at your priorities and what you aspire to do with your time. Scheduling is where these aspirations meet reality. Scheduling is the way for you to look at the time available to you and plan how you will use it to accomplish the tasks you have identified. Through effective scheduling, you can

- Understand which tasks you can realistically accomplish with your time.
- Plan to make the best use of your available time.
- Minimize stress by avoiding over-commitment to yourself and others.

A well thought-out schedule allows you to manage your commitments, still leaving you time to do the things that are important to you. Scheduling is best done continuously, like at the start of every day or week. Start by identifying the time you want to make available for your work. Next, block in the tasks you absolutely must complete to do a good job. These will often be the things you are assessed against. Next, set aside an appropriate contingency time. You will learn how much of this you need by experience.

What you now have left is your discretionary time. This is the time available to deliver your priorities and achieve your tasks. Review your prioritized action list, evaluate the time needed to achieve these tasks, and schedule them in your day or week.

One of the most important ways people learn to achieve success is by maximizing their time. They increase the amount of work they can manage by delegating work to other people, outsourcing key tasks, or using technology to automate as much of their work as possible. This frees them up to achieve their goals.

"A dream is not a revelation. If a dream affords the dreamer some light on himself, it is not the person with closed eyes who makes the discovery but the person with open eyes lucid enough to fit thoughts together."

Michel Leiris

Chapter Eight

Dream Big

Chapter Eight

Dream Big

I believe that each one of us is born with dreams that we are here to discover and experience. Why is it that when we grow up, we forget how to dream? Because we've been programmed to think dreams are for children and adults must give them up to mature. In school we are told to stop day-dreaming and pay attention. They tell us to look at reality and get our heads out of the clouds. Dreams don't pay the bills. Dreaming won't get you anywhere. Do you remember hearing those things when you were in school or at home?

It is not true!

"To think you can create, creates a force that can."
Orison Sweet Marden

While people around us are telling us dreams are unrealistic, we know a dream creates a picture in your mind that is the beginning of what could be realized. If you can see it in your mind, you can make it happen. That's how inventors start out. Every invention that man has developed in history started that very same way. The process has a track record.

The dictionary says that to dream something up is to use your ingenuity in making, developing or achieving what you want. Dreams progress from thought to visualization in your mind to a reality. Don't let other people discourage you from imagining and making it come true.

We waste most of our time in a daily routine that someone else determined for us and feel that we have no direction. Our lack of purpose makes us wonder why we are here. Some of us are able to hold onto our dreams through every experience, positive or negative, but others just give up. You don't have to let go of your dreams.

According to the universal Law of Attraction, you are already bringing people, things and jobs into your life. Once you're aware of it, you can tap into it and intentionally attract things to you. You may be thinking, "Okay, Dana, is it just think positive and sit around waiting, or is there more to it than that? I've heard of this before, but I'm not sure about how it really works."

Let's look at the process you can use. First, have a clear picture of exactly what you want. I have many dreams. I love to travel, experience new things and challenge myself. I enjoy starting new business ventures and seeing them through to completion. Each one of those dreams has a very real picture to go with it. I see myself at a beautiful cabin in the mountains doing all the things I want to there.

Next, focus your thoughts on that picture. Allow yourself to accept it. Don't let yourself get stuck back there when you thought you didn't deserve good things. You do - don't forget that.

"So many of our dreams at first seem impossible, then they seem improbable, and then, when we summon the will, they soon become inevitable."
Christopher Reeve

When you're really focused on your dream, you get excited and build up positive energy and emotions. That creates a kind of vibration that attracts other things with the same vibrations. It's like changing the station on the radio. When the frequency matches up with the numbers you choose, you get the music you could initially hear in your head before you actually heard it. You are literally on the same wavelength. When you're excited, you spread that enthusiasm to others who can feel your emotions. You send out energy and get back the same. Have you ever heard a speaker that motivated you to the point that you wanted to run out and succeed right that minute? That's the feeling I'm talking about.

When it feels good, take action with intent. Even though the universe will be in charge of when and where, you have to take an active part in the process. While you're focusing and doing, you will attract what and who you need to succeed.

"Keep your dreams alive. Understand to achieve anything requires faith and belief in yourself, vision, hard work, determination and dedication. Remember all things are possible for those who believe."

Gail Devers

I dreamed of unlimited wealth and how to help others find it, too. I have been doing that for several years through my past successes and now through my financial planning seminars. When you discover your dream, it creates a passion to see it fulfilled. That's what moves you forward to your purpose. Like uncovering a burning hot desire, your purpose shows you even more of your purpose, why you are here on this planet.

You have permission to dream. Allow yourself to. Don't limit your dreams to small incidental things that you want or need. Get out of the box you've created for yourself. Turn it over, stand on it and look at the view. Everything is within your reach. Remember when you were a small child and had to drag a stool into the kitchen to see the countertop where all the good things to eat were just out of your reach? The first time you saw the wealth available to you and within your grasp was amazing. Feel that again.

You were put on this earth to experience and fulfill your purpose. A seed was planted inside you for those dreams. Now it's time to water that seed and let it grow. Bring it into the light of day and let the light shine.

If you dream small, you experience limitations that you have put on yourself. If you dream big, the sky is the limit. Your dreams don't all have to be material things like a new Mercedes, a mansion on the mountains, or a private yacht, but they could be. They could be helping the homeless find jobs or providing shelters for the hopeless and neglected. If you're thinking you would like to make $30,000 or $70,000 next year, why limit yourself? Dream big. Imagine yourself with a six-figure income this year and a million the next.

"Make use of time; let not advantage slip."
William Shakespeare

Think about it. If all you want is a car that runs, that's all you'll ever have because that's all you ever talk about or look for. The dream and the thought need to become action. You will attract other people and opportunities to you in order to accomplish your goals.

Visualize yourself climbing into that brand new Mercedes and driving it away. See yourself wave to the salesman as you take your dream car off the lot and leave your old jalopy behind. It all starts with becoming aware of the possibilities. Keep breathing and allow yourself to dream in Technicolor.

When you have an idea about who you want to be or what you want to do, you can make the idea the main thing in your life. You think it, dream it and live it. It is the focus in your body, your actions, and your thoughts. Concentrate on that dream and leave other things alone. I found out that is the way some people become great successes and financial giants in their field.

We are responsible for what we become. Our dreams can become reality. We have the power within us to remake ourselves. If we have made ourselves what we are through our desires, dreams, attitudes and actions, we can change our future by focusing on a new and better dream. I learned that I could change my circumstances through a new mindset and the actions that came from that change.

> *"The only difference between dreams and reality is action."*
>
> Dana Neubert

My new journey was not an easy one, but I realized the life I had lead was dark and depressing. I had a deep desire for financial security and continued to push myself forward. I chose to go through the long and tedious process of educating myself.

After three years of hard work and perseverance, I became financially free. My passion continues to be helping others. Each one of us has a dream and a passion that leads to our fulfillment. When you find something that interests you, explore it. Find out everything you can about the subject. Talk to others, read books, watch documentaries, visit the library and ask the reference librarian to help you. Do a Google search on the Internet. Don't limit yourself to one source.

After learning about your subject, how do you know if it's your dream? One way is to ask yourself what you think about when you first wake up in the morning and the last thing you think about at night. What would you rather be doing with your time than how you spend it now? Let yourself get emotional about it. What do you like to talk about? Who do you want to spend your time with? What do you make time for? These questions can help you find out what your burning desires are.

If you explore something and find you're not as interested as you first thought you were, that's okay. Everything you learn gives you more depth. You will be surprised when that knowledge will come in handy. Enjoy the journey. Pick out another interest. Spend time learning about it like you did before. If your dream is working with children, volunteer in an organization that gives you the experience with them. It may surprise you. Let the creativity inside express itself. Remember your thoughts give you direction.

"All you need to do is think a certain way, move into action, think positively, see yourself already having it, move it into action, and attract it into your life."
Bob Proctor

After exploring your interests and your dreams, it's important to look at your natural strengths. Your dreams aren't limited, but if you have no knowledge or experience in environmental science, you probably aren't going to want to be a lab researcher to find a solution for global warming. It is a noble cause, and you may support it with your feelings and donations, but you would need to start at the bottom and be trained for the task.

Your dreams are the ones that come from deep inside and won't go away. One of the biggest obstacles we face is the fear that we can't do it. If other people told us we are failures and never finish anything, we have put that in our belief system, which trips us all the time.

Some people are actually more afraid of succeeding at their goal than they are of failing. What if you get your dream? What if you become a nationally and internationally known speaker? Then what? It might scare you to think about the responsibility to all those people. You begin to doubt your path and wonder why anyone wants to listen to you. You have made your success a stumbling block by your doubts and thoughts.

Go back to visualizing yourself doing well at your dream. See yourself being ready for the daily tasks and knowing the information well enough to share. Trust your experiences and the lessons you've learned. Most people will find something in what you say that is similar to their lives.

A life full of disappointments and loss can make you depressed, and you feel like giving up. You don't have the energy for a dream. This obstacle can stop you in your tracks, but it doesn't have to be permanent. You can work your way out of it one small step at a time. That rebuilds your confidence.

When the obstacles to achieving your dreams seem too big to push through, sit down and breathe. Take a walk in the fresh air to clear your head. Relax in a hot bath for an hour away from all your worries. If you need to work through parts of your past with a professional counselor, include that in your path.

It takes spiritual and emotional strength to dream and to make it happen. One thing that can help you is to visualize what things look like in your life on the other side of the obstacle. If you can't see around it, use the visualizing tool. Remember if you can see it in your mind, you can make it come true.

You need to be intentional about your actions. Be positive, and the things that you need will come to you in the form of a class, a book or a person. Many times what comes to you and helps you along your path may be totally unexpected. You know you will attract what is needed, but you may not be sure exactly what that is. It's like putting together a one thousand piece puzzle. You get down to the last ten or twenty pieces, and the picture is almost finished. You can see most of it, but some of the last pieces don't seem to fit like you thought they would. You know they have to go somewhere, but you aren't sure where. All the things you need to finish are within your reach. A friend with a different perspective can sit down where you are and help you see what to do to complete the picture.

It's sad to think about, but most people will die without ever realizing their dreams. I don't want to do that, and I'm sure you don't, either. You have it within you to dream and make your dream come true.

Focus on what moves you forward to reach your goal. Being emotionally involved in making a better life for others as well as yourself has a bigger payoff than focusing on yourself alone. We're here to make a difference. That's why I hung onto my dream of helping others for so many years when I wasn't even sure how to help myself.

"If one advances confidently in the direction of his dreams and endeavors to live the life which he has imagined, he will meet with a success unexpected in common hours."
Henry David Thoreau

One thing to consider is if you're not moving forward, you're probably moving backward. What is the price of standing still or going backward to you? You may be losing more than just your dream. You may suffer financially or in your relationships with your spouse or children. It may affect your self-esteem.

The universe has a natural flow to the things that happen. It's like going to the Oregon coast and watching the waves come onto the beach or the tides go in and out every day. There is also a natural flow in your life. It comes from your thoughts and actions. Does what you think give off negative or positive energy? You can push away those things that you want or you can attract them to you. It is your choice. We determine how our lives will progress.

Sometimes we give ourselves a timetable of the way things should happen. If it doesn't happen that way, we think we've failed. You haven't, though, because you're still moving toward your dream. We need to be a part of the energy flowing in us and in the universe around us. The universe's timing is usually better than our own and is much more fulfilling. It gives us all what we need. Under our own efforts, we may be missing things along the way.

There are many, many stories about people who have dreamed and then created that dream. Bob Proctor, Zig Ziglar, Donald Trump and Robert Kiyosaki started with a dream of who they could be and what they could do to help other people make a better life for themselves. You can model yourself after the people that you admire. It worked for them, and it can work for you.

"You become what you think about all day."
Earl Nightingale

Chapter Nine

Persistence

Chapter Nine

Persistence

Persistence is defined as the ability to maintain action, regardless of your feelings. Basically, you stick to your plan to achieve your goals even when you feel like quitting. No matter who you are or what circumstance you may be in, at some point in your progress toward a goal, your motivation will be tested. Sometimes you'll feel motivated; sometimes you won't. Remember, however, that your motivation does not produce positive results. Your actions do. Accepting this fact will help you to alter your behaviors in order to maintain motivation. Persistence enables you to keep taking action even when you've lost your motivation, and therefore, you keep accumulating results.

Persistence also acts as a motivating factor for you. By continuing your actions regardless of the immediate outcome, you'll eventually get results, and results can be very motivating.

"Nothing in the world can take the place of Persistence. Talent will not; nothing is more common than unsuccessful men with talent. Genius will not; unrewarded genius is almost a proverb. Education will not; the world is full of educated derelicts. Persistence and Determination alone are omnipotent. The slogan "Press On" has solved and will always solve the problems of the human race."

Calvin Coolidge

It is important to note that persistence is not stubbornness. You develop persistence through self-discipline. Self-discipline makes you take action regardless of your emotional state.

Imagine how your life would change if you could harness the self-discipline to follow through on your goals, no matter what. Self-discipline is a large part of the affirmations and visualizations that we talked about in the last chapter. Picture yourself saying to your body, "You're overweight. Lose twenty pounds." Without self-discipline, that intention won't become a reality. But with good self-discipline, you will lose those twenty pounds in no time. Self-discipline should be applied to every aspect of your life. By doing so, each conscious decision that you make will be virtually guaranteed to come to fruition.

"Anything your mind can conceive and believe it can achieve."

Napoleon Hill

Self-discipline is one of the most important personal development tools that you need to develop. The goals you can accomplish with self-discipline are unsurpassable. It can empower you to take charge of your life and live the one you've always dreamed of. You can lose any amount of weight, make as much money as you want, or overcome any addiction. It can eliminate procrastination, disorder and ignorance. It becomes a powerful force when combined with other tools like the release of past beliefs, affirmations and visualizations, goal-setting and persistence.

How do you develop self-discipline? Just like with exercising, the more you train it, the stronger you become. The less you train it, the weaker you become. Just as everyone has different levels of physical fitness, we all have different levels of self-discipline. Everyone has a little self-discipline. For example, most people get out of bed and go to work on a Monday morning. But not everyone has developed his or her discipline to the same degree. Just as it takes muscle to build muscle, it takes self-discipline to build self-discipline.

Have you ever gone to the gym and lifted weights for the first time? You work your arms, legs and every other muscle in your body, probably lifting too much weight for your first time at the gym. The next morning you are so sore you can't move even your little finger. You are so miserable that you swear off the gym for the rest of your life. Building self-discipline is the same process. The basic method of building self-discipline is tackling challenges near your limit that you can successfully accomplish.

This doesn't mean continuously trying something and failing at it every day, nor does it mean never straying from your comfort zone. You won't gain any strength by trying to lift a weight that is too heavy; nor will you gain strength lifting weights that are too light for you. To effectively build your self-discipline, you must start with challenges that are within your limit. To progressively train for self-discipline, you need to up the ante after each time you succeed. If you fail to challenge yourself in life, you won't gain any more self-discipline.

So don't push yourself too hard when trying to build self-discipline. If you try to change your entire life overnight by setting dozens of new goals for yourself that you expect to follow consistently starting the very next day, you're almost certain to fail.

And don't be embarrassed if you have too little self-discipline. You have to start somewhere, right? You can still use what little discipline you have to build more. The more disciplined you become, the easier life gets. Challenges that were once impossible for you will eventually seem like a walk in the park.

Don't compare yourself to others. It won't help. You'll only find what you expect to find. If you think you're weak, everyone else will seem stronger. If you think you're strong, everyone else will seem weaker. There's no point in doing this. Simply look at where you are now and aim to get better as you go forward.

While my example may be nothing like yours, you still can benefit from my experiences. By increasing your challenges just a little each week, you stay within your capabilities and grow stronger over time. Developing self-discipline benefits you in every step of obtaining your goal. Self-discipline produces something of value and makes you stronger.

Remember earlier when I said that persistence is not stubbornness? So how do you know the difference? Start by asking yourself these questions:

- Is your plan still correct? If the answer is "no," update your plan and move on.
- Is your goal still correct? If not, update or abandon your goal. There's no need to hang on to a goal that no longer inspires you or fits in with your ever-improving life.

This was difficult for me to learn. I had always believed that I should never give up. I thought that once I set a goal, I should hang on to it with every fiber of your being until the bitter end. I suffered tremendous guilt if I ever failed to finish a project or complete a goal.

Fortunately, I discovered that this is just nonsense. If you're experiencing any amount of personal growth, it stands to reason that are going to be a different person each year. And if you consciously aspire to personal development, the changes will often be dramatic and rapid. It is impossible for you to guarantee that the goals you set today will still be ones you'll want to achieve a year from now. Don't let your future slip away by holding onto outdated goals.

You have to either complete or delete your old goals so that you can make room for new ones. Sometimes your new goals are so compelling and inspiring that there's no time to complete old ones. They have to be abandoned half-finished. This has always been uncomfortable for me to do, but I know it's necessary. The hardest part of this process is consciously deciding to eliminate an old goal, knowing it will never be finished. It took me a long time to come to grips with this, but it was necessary for my own growth.

"If I had to select one quality, one personal characteristic that I regard as being most highly correlated with success, whatever the field, I would pick the trait of persistence. Determination. The will to endure to the end, to get knocked down seventy times and get up off the floor saying, 'Here comes number seventy-one!"

Richard M. DeVos

Your pursuit of personal growth, success, and happiness will be a great asset for developing persistence. For example, if all of your life you wanted to be a writer, but you work as an accountant, then you probably will become bored with it after a few years. The value of persistence comes from a vision of the future that's so compelling you would give almost anything to make it real. The vision I have of my future now is far greater than the one I had for five years ago.

"Never give in, never give in; never, never, never, never – in nothing, great or small, large or petty never give in, except to convictions of honor and good sense."

Winston Churchill

Use the space on the next page to identify the parts of your life where persistence can be used to help you fulfill your vision.

Persistence of action comes from persistence of vision. When you have a definite idea about what you want, you'll be consistent in your actions. And that consistency of action will produce consistency of results.

"Success doesn't come to you…you go to it."
Marva Collins

Chapter Ten

Financial Independence

Chapter Ten

Financial Independence

The most obvious step to financial independence is to make more money. The first thoughts that may come into your mind are to either work longer hours at your current job or get a second job. On the surface, these may seem like the most effective ways to increase your cash flow, leading to financial independence, but they are not. I don't believe in trading your time for money and neither should you. Before you can become financially independent, you need to change your mindset about money.

By this I mean that you need to reevaluate the way you look at earning money. Let me explain. Getting a second job or working overtime in your current job will cause you to spend more money on things like childcare. This is a vicious cycle. The following steps will help you to attract more money into your life:

- You must develop a healthy relationship and attitude toward money. The love of money is not greed. It is no different than loving gourmet food. Money merely makes life worth living, and there is nothing wrong with wanting to live a happy life. Imagine your life with more than enough money and all of its benefits. The more you do this, the easier it gets to think of yourself this way too.

- Sit down and create a budget for yourself. First, write out your monthly income. Then on a separate sheet of paper write out your monthly costs and expenses. Create a reasonable budget based on this information.

- Increase Your Income. The most obvious way is to work more hours at the job, but remember how we talked about the problem of trading time for money? Set up multiple streams of income that flow in on an automatic and consistent basis. With multiple streams of income, you won't have to work much more than usual to create more income. You don't have to endure struggle or hardship to increase your income. The key is to view your income-earning potential differently. Believe and you will achieve.

Dispel the Myths

In terms of financial independence, many of us are bound by the "old" beliefs of our parents. Stay out of debt and pay off your house, and you'll be set for life. Sound familiar?

I used to believe that paying off your mortgage was the best way to increase your financial independence. This is not the case for several reasons. One reason is that you need the tax deduction. For many of us, the only tax deduction we get is from our mortgage interest deduction. One of the worst financial mistakes you can make is to drain your available funds by paying off your mortgage. Another reason is that many people believe that their money is safest when it is invested in their home. This is not a good investment because of the real estate booms and busts. Your home equity can disappear with the fluctuations in the market.

All of our lives, we've been told, "A penny saved is a penny earned." That's not necessarily true. Debt isn't always a bad thing. Now, I'm not telling you to go max out your credit cards. But think of it this way; wouldn't you rather have a small amount of debt in student loans and a large sum of money in a savings or money market account? Debt, if used wisely, can be a great financial tool. Donald Trump is a good example of someone who became very wealthy through debt. Debt has tremendous potential to benefit us if used correctly.

Another common myth is to invest in 401Ks and IRAs. Did you know that minimum required distributions trigger a heftier tax bill after age seventy? To avoid this, you should put your money into an investment-grade cash value life insurance policy. If structured correctly, this will provide a steady stream of tax-free cash. Before we go any further, let's define the differences in life insurance choices:

- **Term insurance.** This is the cheapest, simplest kind of life insurance. Buy a policy for a set term (typically 10 or 20 years) and if you die during that time, your beneficiary will receive the benefit.

- **Whole life.** This is the simplest type of permanent life insurance. Your premiums remain the same throughout the life of the policy, and a portion of each premium is invested by the company, allowing you to accumulate this money (the cash value) on a tax-deferred basis.

- **Universal life.** This has the same basic features as whole life, but is a bit more flexible. If you choose, you can pay in amounts above your regular premium, and adjust the death benefit relative to the cash value amount.

- **Variable life.** With a variable policy, you get a choice of different funds where the company will invest your money for you. Generally, if the investments do well you'll have a higher death benefit and greater cash value. It they don't do well, you'll have a lower death benefit and cash value, though some policies guarantee a minimum death benefit.

- **Variable universal life** combines the flexibility of adjusting the amount of the death benefit and premium (as in universal life) with the ability to take a little more risk in investment choices in the hope of getting a bigger return (as in variable life).

Sounds strange, I know. But let me take a moment to explain. You pay the greatest possible premium to buy the least amount of death benefit and the contract still qualifies legally as life insurance. Now, the excess premium (the amount beyond what's needed for the actual insurance) grows tax-deferred, generating cash value.

If you manage this policy properly, this growing cash value can be accessed tax-free through withdrawals that don't exceed the premium paid and/or policy loans in which the interest charged is mostly, if not totally, offset by the interest credited on the cash value. This strategy is perfect, particularly for people who don't want stock market risk and want guarantees. And still another advantage of this is that this allows you to leave a tax-free death benefit to your beneficiaries.

Multiple Streams of Income

Most of us only have one source of income, our current job. Unfortunately, our job never seems to provide us with the amount of money we need to live the life we dream of. But what if you had all the money you desired? One of my first goals was to get a check in the mail every day. Imagine walking to your mailbox that is filled with money. This is possible with multiple streams of income.

What does the phrase multiple streams of income (MSI) mean? MSI is exactly what it implies – income from multiple sources. This is fairly straightforward, but what is meant by "streams" of income? If you and your spouse both have jobs, does that mean you are getting MSI?

Perhaps a two-income family could be classified as MSI, based on the definition that it is more than one income, and it does bring a steady flow of money into your bank account. But that isn't really what we mean when we talk about MSI. MSI includes various investments such as real estate or network marketing.

The universe is overflowing with these opportunities; you just have to be creative enough to find them. Here are a couple of ideas to help boost your creativity:

- Change "multiple" from two to many more (50, 100, 200).
- Change "steady" from once a month to multiple times a day.

Let's take me for example; recently I was expecting a $300,000 return from a real estate transaction. That did not happen because of the mortgage industry. Many years ago, I would have been very upset, but today I realize that when one door shuts another one opens. I am very grateful I did not get that money. Sometimes when I get a large amount of money I get lazy, but now I just pursue other avenues. Because this happened, I met the some of the greatest people in the world. I had to seek out different ways to make money. I have always known what Donald Trump, Robert Kiyosaki (*Rich Dad Poor Dad*) and Bob Proctor did. They did multi-level (MLM) marketing. I was never successful in this industry. In the past, I had tried two other companies and did not make any money. I always thought you had to be a big shot who knew a lot of people, and then I told myself that I was a big shot I changed my mindset..

I researched the best MLM company I could find. I didn't want to sell anything, so the research was difficult. Bob Proctor once told me that my job is first to speak and then to have the most incredible team behind me. I took his advice and went to training for MLM strategies. At the end, a lady asked me if I was excited. My first reaction was that I was not; I just didn't feel like I could be successful at MLM. Later that evening, three people explained the company and opportunity to me. As they explained the process to me, I remembered Bob's words and asked them to join my team.

During the next ten days, we worked to help break every sales record we could. Life is amazing, but through network marketing it is even better. We are now helping all our friends quit their jobs. The greatest thing is to see our friends have hope and transform themselves into the incredible human beings that God designed them to be. I will never give up network marketing. I love helping people transform their lives. Feel free to e-mail me if you would like to be on my team.

An important aspect of MSI is that you want to create "passive" sources of income as often as possible. It is difficult, and sometimes ineffective, to trade time for money, so any form of income you receive shouldn't take a lot of your time or energy. Your goal is to create an environment where you receive money on a regular basis because you contributed in some way but aren't actively involved on a daily basis. Having said that, I want to remind you that you don't get "something for nothing," so you will have to spend some time and energy in the beginning. The amount of time depends on the MSI, but after the start-up phase, it continues to earn money without your direct intervention.

Another important point regarding MSI is that everyone is a contact. No matter the person, they could be a potential source of income for you. Don't jeopardize a potential contact through inappropriate actions. Remember the Golden Rule. "Do unto others as you would have done unto you." You should be professional in all of your dealings. You never know; the cashier at Wal-Mart may be a source of MSI in the future. You are making all kinds of contacts and talking to people every day that can potentially help you or give you ideas for more MSI, and those contacts should be maintained.

Creativity is the key to success with MSIs. Don't concern yourself with what others are doing; try something new that has never been done before. Don't worry about being perfect. All you have to do is give it the best you've got. Every day give your best effort. Dare to live the life you have imagined. Visualize exactly how you want to live; then attempt to live that way. Don't view an MSI as something that's going to happen in the distant future. Instead, look at it as something that already is.

The majority of our financial worries are caused when we try to make decisions before we have sufficient knowledge. We get lost in the negative thinking and the "what ifs." Doubting is a natural instinct, so make a point to eliminate the doubt from your mind. Affirm and visualize the end result and know where you're going in order to get there.

MSIs aren't just about receiving money. I know this sounds strange since we've just been talking about getting checks in the mail everyday, but you need to learn that you must give in order to receive. This theory takes some getting used to partly because the concept, "go out and get," has been ingrained in our minds since childhood. How many times have you been called a "real go-getter?" Before you can truly reach your unlimited income potential, you must change your mindset to one of giving. Givers get. When we project positive energy into the universe, that same positive energy comes back to us, often several times over. You learned in chapter two how to stop letting your old beliefs limit you, and this is true more than ever when we are referring to financial prosperity.

What you earn is an indication of how your subconscious mind is programmed. For example if $45,000 is the most money you have ever earned in a year, that's probably the income level you will stay at. This is because what you earn is an expression of your subconscious, conditioned way of thinking about yourself and your ability to earn money. Now is the time for you to rid yourself of that limiting mindset. In order to manifest MSIs into your life, you want to refocus your thoughts and behaviors to financial abundance by developing new habits and new ways of thinking.

Start doing a little research on the many affiliate programs that are available to anyone and everyone. They are simple to start and don't require any specialized knowledge. It is very important to remember that an MSI isn't a job; it is a passport to a life filled with wealth beyond your wildest imagination.

The Foundation of Multiple Streams of Income

In chapter one, we talked about needing a blueprint to determine where you want to go in life. For MSIs you need a foundation. Think about a skyscraper. These giants stand firm and strong over the streets below, but how do they stand so tall without falling down? Their foundation is carefully designed to support them, just as the foundation of your MSI should be carefully designed to remain strong and consistent. A good deal of thought and effort has been put into the foundation of a building, and your financial foundation shouldn't be any different.

Once a strong foundation is built, the construction of an MSI is easy. If we equate a skyscraper to financial freedom, you will see your wealth rise high into the sky because the stronger the foundation, the more stories of wealth you can add!

To build a strong foundation of wealth, you need to be healthy in four basic areas. To begin with, you have to be physically healthy. If you aren't healthy, you don't have the energy to focus on new opportunities. Exercise regularly because lack of exercise will cause you to have poor immunity and become susceptible to diseases. Exercise enables you to free your mind and concentrate on your goals. You also need to get an adequate amount of sleep. You want to be at your sharpest mentally when planning your financial freedom.

Not only do you need to be physically healthy, but you should also be mentally healthy. Poor mental health inhibits your decision-making and can be very costly. Try meditation. This helps to increase your level of concentration and reduce the risk of making mistakes. Meditation also helps to minimize anything distracting you from your goals.

Meditation also helps with your emotional health. You need to make decisions based on facts, not emotions. If you are unstable emotionally, your judgment is compromised. Practicing mediation will help to calm you and manage your emotions.

If you are terrified of taking a risk, for example, then you will not be able to make the best decisions essential for increasing your wealth. If you can learn to manage your fear of risk, you will be able to make sound decisions and watch your single income grow into MSI.

Earlier in this chapter we talked about the "givers get" philosophy. This is a large part of the final component needed for a foundation of wealth - good spiritual health. This can be anything from helping feed the poor to giving shelter to the homeless or sharing your knowledge with others so that they can have a better life. Donating money isn't the only way to increase your spiritual health. Setting a positive example, showing genuine concern, or listening attentively to someone's needs are also good ways. Through your giving, you will achieve limitless possibilities. Being healthy in these four areas is necessary to lay a strong foundation for an MSI. Once you have a balance between the four, you will be able to maintain a level of financial freedom you once thought to be unattainable.

Steps to Creating Wealth Quickly

The following is a list of suggestions for creating wealth quickly.

- Develop a wealth consciousness. Most of us live with a consciousness of lack. We believe there is only so much wealth to go around, and the majority of it has already been accounted for.

- Combine concepts. Take ideas and technologies from one business and move them into another. Taking two different businesses and combining or merging the concepts can bring an entirely new concept to the marketplace, tapping into a new and untouched source of money.

- Create a perception of value. No matter what the product is, you must always create the perception that it has value. Without being able to see the value in a product or service, most people won't give it a second look. The value of any product or service must outshine those of any of its competitors.

- Learn from your competitors' mistakes. This will enable you to gain an instant strategic advantage in any market you choose to enter.

- Location. Location. Location. This is certainly true for real estate, but it is also true for businesses. Look at successful businesses in your area and move your business into another area where one isn't already in existence.

- Repeat your process. Anytime you find something that works, repeat and duplicate the process on a larger scale. Before you know it, your wealth will grow exponentially.

- Saturate the market with your product or service's name and message. Find a medium such as TV, radio or the Internet to tell everyone about your product or service.

The key to financial independence is to open our minds to new and innovative strategies as well as take advantage of the methods that have stood the test of time such as MSIs. Never forget the one truth. There is no such thing as a limit on your income.

"When you are grateful fear disappears and abundance appears."
Anthony Robbins

Chapter Eleven

Gratitude

Chapter Eleven

Gratitude

In the previous chapters, we discussed positive thinking and attitude. Living with an attitude of gratitude can make all the difference in your world. If we lose sight of it, we give up our focus and our purpose. To do the things I love to do and help others unlock their potential is my purpose. Each morning I sit on the edge of my bed and say out loud, "I am so grateful for this day."

Every day we wake up is another blessing. I am thankful for those things I see and have now, but also for things that are coming to me in my life. You will release the poisons in your system with this kind of attitude. Harboring resentment builds up negativity inside of you. You're the one who pays the biggest price, not the person you're upset with. They may not even be aware of your resentment or choose to ignore it.

"It has been found by experience that a person increases his blessings by being grateful for what he has. Gratitude even on the mental plane is a great magnet. When gratitude is expressed from the spiritual standpoint it is powerfully augmented."

Charles Fillmore

Dwelling on circumstances that aren't going your way builds negative energy. It adds poisons to your mind and body. The obstacle that stops you from becoming the person you want to be and having what you want grows from negativity. Learn to be thankful in all things. You don't have to remain stuck in your discomfort or pain. Begin by being grateful for little things.

If you find yourself in a thought pattern that keeps pulling you down into that old black place, think of one small thing you are glad to have. It might start with, "I'm thankful for a cup of coffee this morning. I'm glad the sun came up again." Then say out loud to yourself anything you can think of that you are grateful for.

You don't like your boss? Be thankful for your job and for the possibilities in your future of the better job you will attract. Talk about your future with your mentor, friends and family. It's not the *someday* that so many people talk about. You can visualize yourself taking an interview and being hired for the job you truly want.

Showing gratitude is recognition of your gifts. Again, it is a verb, not just a noun. It requires action from us. The seed of your actions begins with your thoughts. You can ask for and attract good things into your life.

*"1st Agreement: Be impeccable with your word.
Speak with integrity. Say only what you mean.
Avoid using the word to speak against yourself or
to gossip with others. Use the power of your
word in the direction of truth and love."*

Don Miguel Ruiz

One of the biggest challenges in being thankful in all things is the energy we carry in the old tapes playing in our heads. We forget that all the experiences in our past, both positive and negative, make us who we are today. What is important is how we handle them. Do we choose to continue to poison ourselves or expel the toxins by developing a new attitude of gratitude?

The thoughts I put into my mind determined what I saw as my results. It was up to me how I acted when faced with an obstacle. Even though I changed my way of thinking, the problem still seemed to loom large over me. The difference was that my perception changed. I changed from inside. I let my spirit out and practiced being grateful for all experiences. Sometimes I needed to remind myself to be grateful, but it eventually became a new habit.

The process led me to a place of understanding the role of gratitude in my daily life. My new way of thinking released a power to see things in a brighter light. One of my favorite affirmations is to say, "This is the greatest day ever because my feet are above ground, and I am alive and well." Every morning I begin my day with this saying.

The more I studied about gratitude and how it could affect my future, I was amazed. I found out that it is potentially in all of us. It doesn't depend on genetics. It can be developed by everyone. If you've experienced difficult times as a kid, you can still become a grateful person. We all seem to have a set of positive characteristics and a set of negative ones. We can choose to use either one. Our choice is wrapped up in how we look at our past and present experiences. Were they "good" or "bad?" By the way, deciding if something is "good" or "bad" is a judgment that we make.

I had to find a balance for myself between knowing that I could attract good things into my life and being aware that good things can also come my way through other people. If I get out of balance with that, I have a hard time being grateful to others for what they do that affects me.

Most of us look at our pasts in one of two ways. Unfortunately, more of us see failures, trials and disappointments. We get it the habit of staying in that mindset. That colors our view of the future. We see more of the same. The future is filled with more hassles to endure, more disappointments and other problems to solve. We hear people say, "Life is a bitch, and then you die" or "Life is a vale of tears." How depressing.

On the other hand, others look back and see joy, success and experiences that enriched their lives. Twins could look at the same circumstances from two different viewpoints. The person who looks back on his life and sees things in a positive way will see his future as one of satisfaction and success. It all starts and ends with an attitude of gratitude. This gratitude is one of the quickest ways I've found to start the Law of Attraction working in my life.

So start keeping a journal to be aware of the things you are grateful for. It shouldn't just be a list of things that make you happy, which is okay, but you can learn to be grateful even in tough times. Remember, it is the attitude we're after. The concept of gratitude doesn't mean that you have to be happy in every circumstance. It doesn't mean staying in your current situation and finding something to be glad about. Some people might think that this new attitude can make you passive and somehow content no matter what your circumstances. That isn't what I'm trying to say. If your surroundings and your friends need to be changed for you to have a better life, then by all means do what you need to do. I did. You can too with the help of others to support you.

One simple daily practice is a way to begin putting the attitude of gratitude to work. Say a short prayer of thankfulness at a meal; it can be out loud with your family or silently to yourself. It acknowledges the fact that you have something to eat. Start with simple things and your awareness of all the gifts you have in your life will become clearer.

As I learn more and help people by sharing my past, I realize that I have been given many possibilities. I am the one that needs to take the action needed and move forward. I realize that it is a choice to have gratitude as a main focus in my life.

When we go through difficult times, we can learn to be thankful that we have the strength to get through them. It helps us to get over things and move on. Hard times are only temporary. It's helpful to remember that little nugget. The good thing about being grateful when things are going well is that it helps us enjoy it all the more.

*"To educate yourself for the feeling of gratitude
means to take nothing for granted, but to always
seek out and value the kind that will stand behind
the action. Nothing that is done for you is a
matter of course. Everything originates in a will for
the good, which is directed at you. Train yourself
never to put off the word or action for
the expression of gratitude."*

Albert Schweitzer

When I look back on all the experiences I went through as a single mother, I can see that a lot of my problems were because of my attitude. Changing your negative outlook doesn't happen just because your mom or dad tells you to get a new one. It took me a long time to develop the "I don't care" and "don't push me" attitudes I carried around all the time. To make things worse, I blamed everyone else for my bad attitude.

At the time, I had no idea that my own lack of gratitude and my defensive attitude caused so many of my problems with people. I would get into a bad situation that I thought I had to fight my way out of and then wonder why bad stuff always happened to me. I felt that other people pushed me into behaving badly. It took me a long time to learn that what I thought and what kind of attitude I showed to everyone around me made a huge difference in my life.

I have also learned that my attitude has a lot to do with my experiences. How you respond to something is more important than what happens to you. You get to choose whether you have a bad attitude or one of gratitude.

Your attitude is more important than your experiences as a kid, at school, in sports or at home. Your attitude is more significant than what has happened to you in the past, how much money you made from your last job, or how big your house used to be. A good attitude is more important than past failures or successes. It's not just how you dress, what car you drive or how skilled in something you might be. If your attitude is one of gratitude, you are always thankful for something. That creates positive energy and helps you attract abundance to you for now and the future, no matter what your past has been like.

The good thing about your attitude is you get to decide what kind you want. You have complete control of how you act and what kind you want to keep. Every day when I get up, I choose to be grateful for my family and blessings.

If we depend on others or blame them for our attitudes or moods, we give up our own power to create things from within our spirit. Other people are going to act how they want to, but we don't have to be controlled by them. We can decide to have a grateful attitude no matter what the circumstances are.

I've learned over the years that life is partly what happens to me. Most of it is how I react to what happens. Instead of letting it make me feel bad or angry, I can react to it how I want. I can look for the lesson or the blessing in the experience and be thankful. Believe me; if I can change my attitude from the dark places I used to be all the time, you can too. You are in charge of what your attitude is every day. It's not anybody else's fault. Don't let other people tell you how to feel or how to act. Develop the attitude of gratitude, and you will have a more blessed and abundant life.

If you have gratitude in your daily life, you will be much happier. You can walk around feeling miserable, or you can be a happy and stronger person. It takes as much effort to be miserable as to be happy, so why not just choose to be thankful?

You might think it sounds strange to say the work is the same for both attitudes, but look at this way; you use the same amount of energy to say something nice as to say something negative. Sometimes, it probably takes more energy to stay negative when good things are happening.

This change in the way you think is not automatic. It will take some effort on your part, but it is well worth it. Like playing a sport or a musical instrument, the more you practice the better you become. It will unlock potential inside of you that you may not be aware of yet.

"There is no scarcity of opportunity to make a living at what you love. There is only a scarcity of resolve to make it happen."
Wayne Dyer

To move forward in your path, you need to move from thoughts, to words, to feelings and finally to actions. When you're moving forward, it is with a positive and thankful attitude that starts in your mind and spirit. You look for how to accomplish something you want, rather than being stuck with negative thoughts. You choose not to just sit down and say to yourself that what you want can't happen. It can be done. There are steps to get what you want. Gratitude for what you have and for what you are bringing into your life are important parts of that process.

Some people don't understand the idea of being thankful for something you don't even have yet. We've talked about visualizing your dreams. Think about each thing that you will do to accomplish that goal. See yourself reading and listening to financial books that help you on your path. Be thankful that these books are available. Don't get caught up in lack. So what if you don't have the books in your house? Go to the library or share with a friend. Go on the Internet. Be grateful for the options.

You live in an abundant world with more things available to you than you can imagine. They are there for you to use and have. You may be thinking, "But Dana, you don't know what I've been through. You're different. It's easy for you to attract wonderful things into your life and the money to have what you want." That is exactly what I'm talking about; you are looking at life in a negative way. You are coming from a place of lack and hopelessness.

We can't always control what happens to us. Some experiences are circumstances beyond our control because of what others around us do. The big difference I want to share with you is that you have total control of how you react and what kind of attitude you are going to have about it. You get better at it with time. Then, you will be in charge of the changes going on in your life instead of having changes put on you from outside. Scott Hamilton, the Olympic Skater, overcame physical problems in his life. He once said, "The only disability in life is a bad attitude."

It is all about you deciding to have a positive and grateful attitude. You bring it to your life and share it with others. It's not about the negative experiences or things that life has brought to you in the past. It is your state of mind. You decide on the attitude you bring to everything. The more you learn to be thankful, the easier it will be to see things you can be grateful about.

Don't concentrate on what you don't want, but on what you do want. Put in writing your own affirmations about what you want. Write them down as if you are grateful that they are already your life. The attitude of gratitude will make a huge change in how you feel when you get up in the morning and when you go to bed at night. People around you will ask what's different about you. They will say, "What's going on? You're different than you used to be. You're so much better off than you used to be." It is in your reach to develop and use gratitude in your everyday life.

About The Author

Dana Neubert has a Bachelor's of Science degree in Education and currently resides in Centennial Colorado with her family. Dana is a financial advisor and a successful real estate investor with properties across the United States valued at over $11,000,000. In two and a half years Dana was able to acquire multiple businesses and subsequently become financially independent.

As the owner of DanMar seminars, she travels extensively to speak on the issues of financial freedom and multiple streams of income. Through her vast knowledge and expertise, Dana has developed a comprehensive program to teach others how to acquire wealth. In her spare time, Dana volunteers to help raise and train guide dogs for the blind.

You can reach Dana Neubert by email:
beach917@msn.com

SHARE THIS MESSAGE

Bulk Discounts
Discounts start at a low number of copies, ranging from 30% to 50% off based on the quantity chosen.

Custom Publishing
Would you like a private label? or a customization to suit your needs. We could even highlight specific chapters.

Sponsorship
Would you like to sponsor this book? It's a great way to advertise your product or service in a unique way!

Dynamic Speakers
Authors are available to you, to share their expertise at your event!

Call LifeSuccess Publishing at 1-800-473-7134 or email
info@lifesuccesspublishing.com for more information

OTHER BOOKS FROM LifeSuccess Publishing

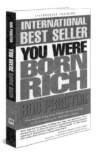

You Were Born Rich

Bob Proctor
ISBN # 978-0-9656264-1-5

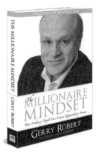

The Millionaire Mindset
*How Ordinary People Can
Create Extraordinary Income*

Gerry Robert
ISBN # 978-1-59930-030-6

Rekindle The Magic In
Your Relationship
Making Love Work

Anita Jackson
ISBN # 978-1-59930-041-2

Finding The Bloom of
The Cactus Generation
*Improving the quality of
life for Seniors*

Maggie Walters
ISBN # 978-1-59930-011-5

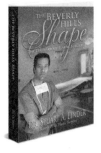

The Beverly Hills Shape
The Truth About Plastic Surgery

Dr. Stuart Linder
ISBN # 978-1-59930-049-8

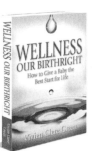

Wellness Our Birthright
*How to give a baby the best
start in life.*

Vivien Clere Green
ISBN # 978-1-59930-020-7

Lighten Your Load

Peter Field
ISBN # 978-1-59930-000-9

Change & How To
Survive In The New
Economy
*7 steps to finding freedom
& escaping the rat race*

Barrie Day
ISBN # 978-1-59930-015-3

Other books from LifeSuccess Publishing

Stop Singing The Blues
10 Powerful Strategies For Hitting The High Notes In Your Life

Dr. Cynthia Barnett
ISBN # 978-1-59930-022-1

Don't Be A Victim,
Protect Yourself
Everything Seniors Need To Know To Avoid Being Taken Financially

Jean Ann Dorrell
ISBN # 978-1-59930-024-5

A "Hand Up", not a "Hand Out"
The best ways to help others help themselves

David Butler
ISBN # 978-1-59930-071-9

Doctor Your Medicine Is Killing Me!
One Mans Journey From Near Death to Health and Wellness

Pete Coussa
ISBN # 978-1-59930-047-4

I Believe in Me
7 Ways for Woman to Step Ahead in Confidence

Lisa Gorman
ISBN # 978-1-59930-069-6

The Color of Success
Why Color Matters in your Life, your Love, your Lexus

Mary Ellen Lapp
ISBN # 978-1-59930-078-8

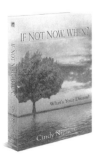

If Not Now, When?
What's Your Dream?

Cindy Nielsen
ISBN # 978-1-59930-073-3

The Skills to Pay the Bills... and then some!
How to inspire everyone in your organisation into high performance!

Buki Mosaku
ISBN # 978-1-59930-058-0

Other books from LifeSuccess Publishing

The Secret To Cracking
The Property Code
*7 Timeless Principles for
Successful Real Estate
Investment*

Richard S.G. Poole
ISBN # 978-1-59930-063-4

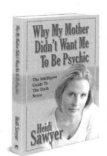

Why My Mother Didn't
Want Me To Be Psychic
*The Intelligent Guide To The
Sixth Sense*

Heidi Sawyer
ISBN # 978-1-59930-052-8

The Make It Happen Man
*10 ways to turn obstacles
into stepping stones without
breaking a sweat*

Dean Storer
ISBN # 978-1-59930-077-1

Change your body
Change your life
*with the Fittest Couple in
the World*

Matt Thom &
Monica Wright
ISBN # 978-1-59930-065-8

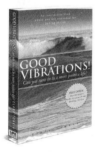

Good Vibrations!
*Can you tune in to a more
positive life?*

Clare Tonkin
ISBN # 978-1-59930-064-1

The Millionaire Genius
*How to wake up the money
magic within you.*

David Ogunnaike
ISBN # 978-1-59930-026-9

Scoring Eagles
*Improve Your Score In Golf,
Business and Life*

Max Carbone
ISBN # 978-1-59930-045-0

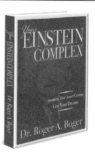

The Einstein Complex
*Awaken your inner genius,
live your dream.*

Dr. Roger A. Boger
ISBN # 978-1-59930-055-9